THE CHILDREN'S PLUTARCH

TALES OF THE ROMANS

NUMA & THE NYMPH·

THE CHILDREN'S PLUTARCH

TALES OF THE ROMANS

BY

F. J. GOULD

illustrated by Walter Crane

YESTERDAY'S CLASSICS

CHAPEL HILL, NORTH CAROLINA

This edition, first published in 2007 by Yesterday's Classics, is an unabridged republication of the work originally published by Harper & Brothers in 1910. For a complete listing of the books published by Yesterday's Classics, please visit www.yesterdaysclassics.com. Yesterday's Classics is the publishing arm of the Baldwin Project which presents the complete text of hundreds of classic books for children at www.mainlesson.com under the editorship of Lisa M. Ripperton and T. A. Roth.

ISBN-10: 1-59915-163-4

ISBN-13: 978-1-59915-163-2

Yesterday's Classics
PO Box 3418
Chapel Hill, NC 27515

CONTENTS

INTRODUCTION

I DO not know why it is that among the Greeks and Romans who are so nearly fabulous as to be scarcely historical at all, Romulus should have a living hold upon the imagination, and Theseus should remain a very dim memory. The Lives of Plutarch begin with these founders of the Roman and the Grecian states, but if the balance tilts so heavily on the side of the Romans, it is dressed in favor of the Greeks in the next following lives of Lycurgus and Numa, and the next of Solon and Poplicola, and the fourth pair, Themistocles and Camillus. It is not until we come to Pericles and Fabius that the balance begins to be even again; and there the splendor of the Grecian's statesmanship eclipses the glory of the Roman patriot in the eyes of those who value civic genius above military virtue.

Of course in the long-run the Romans excel the Grecians in the number of their famous men, but the children ought to remember that the years of Rome were nearly ten times as many as those of Greece; and when their minds kindle with the thought of the Romans who were great from the earliest days of the city far down into the dark of the dying empire, they should be made to consider how glorious the fewer Greeks were in the few short centuries which compassed in time the rise and fall of their republics. As they read Mr. Gould's stories from Plutarch they should be reminded that both Greece and Rome were republican after a brief time, when they were misruled by tyrants, until that long, long time when they sank again under the sway of kings and emperors; the long time which continues yet for most of the European states, but has ceased throughout the whole of America except in the democratic Dominion of Canada. Yet they should be taught that the Roman republic was always a state where even without kings the few ruled the many as they do in Spanish America now, while in the Grecian republics the whole people came nearer the likeness of our own people in their self-government. The freedom of both these states, they should also be taught, was based upon the bondage of men who might be killed or whipped and put to the cruelest shame at the pleasure of their masters because they had suddenly, while free, rich, learned citizens of their native countries, been taken in war, or stolen and sold by pirates. The children should be told that such an immortal sage as Plato was bought for a hundred dollars, and Epictetus, whose philosophy was the study of the good and wise Emperor Marcus Aurelius, was a slave with all the chances of a slave's misery. Not all of the Greeks and Romans were blind to the despair which underlay their highest and bravest hopes, and when Christianity came to them it brought liberty to their bondsmen long after they had lost their own free citizenship.

I believe that if the children realize this they will the more perfectly realize the nobleness and greatness of the Romans whose lives are told in this book. It will be well for them to understand that human nature is a mixed and contradictory thing, and that out of the warring good and evil in it the good often triumphed. Socrates truly said that a slave could have no virtues, and yet the slave Epictetus taught in his book and in his life all the virtues. The young readers should also be made to see how, in every time, human nature has continued capable of the same results; and how very modern in the high things the civilized Greeks and Romans were, while in the low things they remained savage. It will be curious and instructive for them to note how, in the earliest and strongest of the Grecian states, one of the latest dreams of government had come true. The Sparta which the laws of Lycurgus created was a state in which the people were equal sharers in the rights and duties of all; none were rich or poor, except as the others were, and that each did everything for the common weal. But this was for the common weal in war, while the new dream of a perfect state is for the common weal in work, where there are neither rich nor poor in an equality of the peaceful ownership of the land and the tools and the fruits of labor by all, for all.

Another thing which I could wish the children to observe is how the wisest and best of the ancients were in the bonds of fear to signs and portents which men laugh at now. This was because their education was, at the best, philosophical, and dealt with conduct through the discussion of moral principles under gods who had none, while the modern education is scientific, and has enlarged the world to boundlessness through vaster knowledge and sympathy with every form of life. The Roman world, though it was the whole civilized world, was a small world, and it sank at last under the fears and dangers that always encompassed it in the unknown beyond it.

But while it lasted for well a thousand years, what a glorious world it was, and what quenchless memories it has left! It makes one a boy again to think of Romulus and Remus and their wolf foster-mother and the undying city they founded; of the patriots, who drove out the race of kings; of Cincinnatus, who left his plough to serve his country and went back to it when his country was safe; of Regulus, whom the Carthagenians sent to counsel peace to the Romans, but who counselled war, and then held himself bound in honor to return to captivity and death in Carthage; of Virginius, who slew his child rather than let her live the slave of the tyrant; of the stern Brutus, who put his sons to death for treason; of that other Brutus, who joined in slaying his adoptive father, the mighty Cæsar, "because he was ambitious" of the rule of Rome; of the mighty Cæsar himself, with his splendid soldiership and statesmanship; of the warrior and orator Antony; of the stern patriot Cato; of the great Augustus; of the good emperors who made the best of their bad business of being absolute sovereigns.

But I hope that the boys of this present day will see these captains and patriots with clearer eyes than the boys of the past, and will perceive that if their deeds had been done for the help and not for the hurt of others, they would have been far truer and grander heroes. When they read of the last days of the Roman Republic and the first days of the Roman Empire, let them remember how it was that then the spirit of Christ came into the world to bring peace on earth and good-will to men, and to teach the patriotism which is not bound by a city or a country, by a tribe or a nation, but devotes itself to the happiness of all mankind.

W. D. HOWELLS.

PREFACE

IT appeared to me that, by way of preliminary to lessons on justice, government, political progress, etc., it would be well to create in the child-nature a sympathy for some definite historic movement. With this sympathy as a basis, one could better build up conceptions of social justice, civic evolution, and international relations. I could think of no finer material for this purpose than the admirable biographies of Plutarch; though the national history, or the history of Western Europe generally, would doubtless serve the same end. Western history, however, derives its traditions from Greece and Rome, and it seemed to me an advantage to use a work which not only furnished simple instruction in the meaning of politics, but also held rank as a literary classic. My version is intended for children aged about ten to fourteen, after which period they should be encouraged to go direct to the wise, manly, and entertaining pages of Plutarch himself. The spirit of my selection from Plutarch's ample store is aptly represented in the beautiful drawings by Mr. Walter Crane.

F. J. GOULD.

BIOGRAPHICAL NOTE

THE famous author, philosopher, and educator who is known to us as Plutarch—in Greek, Πλουταρχος—was born at Chæronea, in Bœotia, about A.D. 46. The wealth of his parents enabled him to enjoy a thorough education at Athens, particularly in philosophy. After making various journeys, he lived for a long time in Rome, where he lectured upon philosophy and associated with people of distinction, and took an important part in the education of the future Emperor Hadrian. The Emperor Trajan gave him consular rank, and Hadrian appointed him Procurator of Greece. It was about A.D. 120 that he died in his native town of Chæronea, where he was archon and priest of the Pythian Apollo.

In addition to his most famous work, the *Parallel Lives*, known familiarly as *Plutarch's Lives*, he was the author of some eighty-three writings of various kinds. The *Lives*, which were probably prepared in Rome, but finished and published late in life at Chæronea, were intended to afford studies of character, and the vividness of the mental and moral portraiture has made them continue to be a living force. Historically they have supplied many deficiencies in knowledge of the times and persons treated in his great work.

THE TWINS

THE cattle were feeding on the pasture, but the master was not there. He was going toward the river, and he was carrying a burden in his arms. When he reached the edge of the stream he paused. The water ran toward the Mediterranean Sea, rough and noisy.

"I shall not put them straight into the water," he said to himself; "I will leave them here, and perhaps the river will rise and carry them away."

It did. As the flood crept round the wooden trough or cradle, it rocked and then floated. Inside the trough lay two lovely and chubby boy-babes—twins—princes. Their uncle had taken their father's land and theirs, and had bidden the herdsman drown the twins.

The flood of the river Tiber carried the cradle to a green spot, where grew a wild fig-tree. The box lay on the grass, and when the flood went down it still stayed on land. And behold (or you will behold these things if you believe the ancient tale!), a big she-wolf came and gazed at the babes with her fierce and shifty eyes, and she seemed to think they were little cubs that needed her milk, and so she fed them. As they grew older, and were able to toddle about, and were too old for wolf's milk, they got food from a friendly woodpecker. I cannot say whether the woodpecker, with his long beak and tongue, brought the boys food such as he ate himself (that would be insects and grubs), or whether he was good enough to bring berries and other fruits. After a while, however, the herdsman took charge of the boys altogether, and saved the woodpecker any further trouble.

The twins became stout, tall, and strong young fellows, who minded cattle for the chieftain Amulius. One day a loud cry was heard.

"Our cattle have been stolen!"

"Who has taken them?"

"The herdsmen of the chieftain Numitor."

"Follow us!" shouted the tall twins; "we will get them back again!"

A furious fight took place. The twins won. The cattle were brought back in triumph. Then the brothers knew that more war would follow. They joined company with runaway slaves and other people who had no settled homes. These people looked upon the twins—Romulus and Remus—as captains. But Remus was captured, and taken to the house of Numitor.

The herdsman went to Romulus and said:

"Your brother is in danger of death. He will perhaps be killed by his grandfather Numitor."

"I never knew Numitor was our grandfather," replied Romulus.

"Yet it is so. Your mother was his daughter. But Amulius took the power, and wanted to get rid of you two boys, and bade me leave you in the cradle on the river Tiber, where you would soon have been drowned. But it happened otherwise, and I brought you up after a wolf and a woodpecker had fed you."

"I can hardly believe you."

"Well, here is the box you and Remus sailed in. Take it at once to Numitor. Tell him who you are. Perhaps he will spare Remus's life."

Romulus ran straightway to the house of the chief, burst into the room where he was questioning poor Remus, showed the cradle, and told all the strange story. And Numitor, looking at the faces of the young men, saw a likeness to his daughter, and felt sure the tale was true. The two brothers went off with a band of armed men to punish their great-uncle Amulius. Before the little army walked several standard-bearers, carrying poles, on the tops of which were fastened bunches of grass and shrubs. An attack was made on the tyrant's house, and Amulius was slain.

The two young chiefs—for such they now were—made up their minds to build a city of their own. They ploughed with a share or blade drawn by an ox, and ploughed a furrow in a sort of circle. This circle was the line on which the walls were built. But Remus never builded. He had told Romulus that the city ought to be built in another and safer spot.

"If you build here," he said, "the enemy will easily enter—as easily as this."

So saying, he jumped over the ploughed line in a mocking manner.

3

In anger Romulus and his friends fell upon Remus and struck him, and he died. When his passion cooled, great was the sorrow of Romulus; but it was too late; his brother was dead. The city that was being built would now be called after the brother who was left alive—Rome.

On a hill near Rome you could see huts, in which dwelt the men who had joined Romulus, because they had nowhere else to go—slaves who had escaped from their lords, men who had slain neighbors and dreaded being punished by their tribe. After a time you could notice that the folk were divided into classes. First came Romulus the chieftain; he sat on a chair of state; his coat was of purple, and a purple cloak hung over his shoulders. As he walked through the new city, the lictors marched before him, bearing bundles of rods and thongs of leather. If Romulus ordered any man to be beaten, the lictors beat the offender with the rods. If he said "Bind that man prisoner," they bound the person with the leather thongs or straps.

A hundred older men, called the Fathers, or Patricians (*Pat-rish´-ans*), sat together in a council or senate.

The young men who were strong and quick were chosen for soldiers—on foot or horseback.

Certain men would watch birds flying, and if the birds flew in a particular manner they would say:

"It is not the right time to begin a war"—or whatever the purpose might be.

If the birds flew in what they thought a better way, the watchers would say:

"The time is good. The war may begin," or "The house may be built," etc.

These men were called Augurs, and were a kind of priests. Thus we see the classes—the King, the Fathers, the Soldiers, the Priests. The rest were known as the People.

A great feast was held one day. Romulus sat on a throne, dressed in purple. The Romans had asked another tribe, called Sabines (*Sab-ins*), to come to the merry-making, and the Sabines had come, with many maidens, who were ready to dance with the young men of Rome. Suddenly Romulus stood up, and folded his cloak about him.

A shout arose. The Roman young men rushed among the Sabines, and each seized hold of a maiden, and dragged her away to the city, while the Sabine men were held back from interfering. I almost think the young ladies had been told beforehand what would be done, and perhaps they had agreed to be carried away. The story goes on to tell that the Roman young men married the Sabine young women. Romulus had made this plan for the capture, for he thought it was of little use to have a city with so few women in it. For without the women, how could there be true homes?

Wars went on between Romans and Sabines for some years. At last a day came when each side had fiercely attacked the other; each had fled; each had begun the fight again. A crowd of women ran in between the armies. Their hair was disordered; they uttered loud cries. Some carried their babies. Some knelt on the ground, and wept over the bodies of the dead. And one woman spoke for the rest:

"O men, do you wish to hurt us women still more? We were carried away from our fathers and brothers. And now what do we see? Our fathers and brothers are in deadly quarrel with our husbands. Whoever is killed is a lost friend to us. This war robs us of our husbands and our brothers and fathers. We beseech you to stop."

And the Romans and Sabines heard the prayer of the women and made peace, and became one people. How happy it would be if all the tribes of the earth to-day did likewise! And you girls who read this page must help in the making of peace all over the world.

But one woman was not so noble. Before the peace-making of which I have just told you, the Sabines once laid siege to Rome, and a Roman woman named Tarpeia (*Tar-pee-a*) told the enemy she would open the gate to them by night, if they would give her the bracelets of gold which they wore on their left hands. They agreed. She opened the gate, the Sabines ran in. But they did not respect the traitor. The Sabine chief threw at her his bracelet and his shield (which was on his left arm). All the others did likewise, and the false woman sank under a heavy pile of shields and bracelets, and died. And, after all, the Sabines did not win.

Romulus ruled his city for a long time. One day, when he stood among the people in an assembly, the sky became dark, thunder rolled, and all was tempest. Then the sky cleared to brightness. But Romulus could nowhere be seen. People said the gods had taken him away. Of course, this is only a legend.

Not long after that, when the people were gathered together at the place where the senate sat, a senator walked in, and cried:

"O people, I have seen Romulus!"

"Tell us where and how?"

He then told the following story.

He had met Romulus, dressed in bright armor, on the road near the city.

"Why, O King, did you leave the people who loved you?"

"My good friend, I dwelt on earth and built a city, and did my work, and now the gods have called me to heaven. Farewell. Go and tell the Romans that by the exercise of temperance and courage they shall become the greatest people in the world."

WHAT THE FOREST LADY SAID

UP the path among the trees climbed the King. On each side of him, and overhead, the trees spread a thick shade. There was scarce a sound in the mountain forest except the sigh of the wind and the murmur of the brook.

The King's name was Numa. He sat down on a boulder of rock, beside a big pool of water. From one point in the pool the stream ran out and splashed down the hill.

The water trembled. Numa watched it very closely. A lady, clad in forest green, rose up from the pool, and smiled at the King, and sat on one of the rocks. This was not the first time he had met her. Often he visited this spot, and sat talking with the nymph *(nimf)* of the forest.

"Well, Numa," she said, "did you catch the two goblins?"

"Yes; I went to the fountain you told me of, and poured wine into it. When the two goblins came to drink—"

"What did they look like, Numa?"

"One looked like a funny little old man of the woods, with a goat's beard, and the other looked like a woodpecker. They drank of the water, and the wine got into their heads, and made them go to sleep. Then I crept up and caught them both, one in each hand."

"Did they get away?"

"Not till they had told me the charm against thunder, and also the magic way to see into the future, and know what is about to happen."

"What was the charm?"

"They said I was to mix up three strange things into a sort of paste—onions, hair, and the heads of sprats; and if I ate some of it, I should be shielded from the harm of lightning and thunder, and be able to tell the future."

"Very good, Numa; and have the Pontiffs mended the bridge over the river Tiber?"

"Yes; they have set men to work, and had new beams of wood fixed in the bridge to make it strong against the rush of the water. And the Romans are not now afraid to cross the bridge."

"Do the people obey the Pontiffs?"

"Yes; the other day the Pontiffs said the Romans were to hold a holiday, and do no work at all; and every workman in the city stopped his hammer, saw, and other tools. And when they said it was time to sow seed in the corn-fields the people did so."

"That is right. And do the four Fire-Maidens attend to their duty?"

"They do. I have had them dressed in white, as you told me, and they keep the fire burning on the altar day and night, so that the Roman folk may always feel safe. And whenever the Fire-Maidens pass through the streets of the city, the officers carry the bundles of rods in front of them. And last week one of them was being carried in her chair through the city, and there passed by a man who was to be put to death for evil-doing. We spared the man's life because he had met the Vestal maiden."

"That is what I told you to do. And have you built the house for the twenty Heralds?"

"Yes, Lady. If we have any quarrel with any tribe, we shall not think of going to war unless the Heralds give us leave."

"Have you made the eleven shields?"

"I have had them made by a clever smith. He copied very carefully the one which fell from the sky, and which the gods sent us. They look so alike, you could not tell which was the gift of the gods and which are copied. Well, I have chosen twelve lively young men to wear them, and to perform the dance. What did you tell me they were to do?"

"This is the manner of the dancing, Numa. You know it can only be done in one particular month—"

"Yes, the month of March, in honor of the great Mars, the lord of war."

"That is so, Numa. The twelve young men must wear purple jackets and shiny brass belts and brass helmets. They must carry short swords, and, as they leap along the street, they must keep time by beating the shields with short swords."

"The show will please the Romans."

"Yes, Numa, and it will cause them to remember that the city is strong, not by its walls, but by its brave men, who carry shield and sword for the defence of Rome, and are ready to lay down their lives for their brethren."

"And now, Lady, I want to ask you how to stop the people from going on one another's lands, because they often—"

"Not to-day, Numa. I have talked with you enough this time. It is good to talk. It is also good not to talk. And you must now go and see the forest-maiden who puts her finger on her lip. You will find her under yonder fig-tree."

So Numa walked to the fig-tree, and sat under its shady boughs. A lady sat there with her finger on her lips, to show that no one must speak in her presence. She looked into the depths of the forest, as if she was very deeply thinking. Numa did as she did. He kept still, and thought of all the advice which the nymph of the pool had given him; and of the city of Rome; and of the Pontiffs, and the Heralds, and the Fire-Maidens, and the Leapers; and of the people in the many houses of the city, and of the best rules for keeping order, so that all men might be content and do their daily work in peace.

The woodpecker pecked at the trees, but Numa did not hear. And the squirrel jumped from bough to bough, but the sound it made did not reach Numa. At last the Lady of Silence rose up and went away, and the King of Rome also rose, and went down the hill and home to his royal house.

Again Numa went to the pleasant nook in the forest, and again he met the Lady of the Fountain.

"You asked me last time, Numa, how to stay the people from going on each other's lands—from trespassing. Now I will tell you."

"I thank you, nymph of the forest."

"On the border-line between two farms or gardens a hole must be dug. In the hole let the folk pour the blood of an animal that has been slain for the gods. Sprinkle the hole with wine, and honey, and the seeds of plants, and sweet-smelling powders. Then let a big stone be dressed with ribbons and flowers. The stone must be placed in the hole so that it stands upright above the soil. Other stones are to be set at other points in the boundary."

"We will obey your command, Lady."

"And if, O Numa, any man tries to deceive his neighbor, and pulls up the landmark out of the earth, and moves it to another spot, so as to make his own plot of land larger, then a curse shall be uttered upon the man and upon his cattle."

"Yes, he shall be cursed."

"And whoso finds the man may slay him, and to kill the false person shall not be counted murder."

"It is dreadful, but it shall be done."

"And every year, in the month of February, a feast shall be held. The neighbors on each side of the boundary shall come together, with their wives, their children, and their slaves, and shall lay flowers on the stones, and offer cakes to the god Terminus. It shall be a good thing for the folk to meet in peace, and pay respect to the landmarks, and bear in mind that no man ought to take his neighbor's property."

"There is another matter I wish to ask about. The Romans and the Sabines dwell in the same city, but are not always friends."

"Do this, Numa. Tell all the shoemakers to live in the same part of the town, whether they are Romans or Sabines. They will have a company or society of their own, and meet in a hall to make rules for the trade of the shoemakers. And likewise shall the musicians do, and the tanners, the goldsmiths, the masons, the dyers, the brass-workers, the potters, and all the others."

"I will do so. Besides this, Lady, I want to make a better reckoning of the days and months."

"How many months are there in a year, Numa?"

"Ten."

"Yes, but now you must have twelve. Up till now you began the year with March—the month of the Leapers; and the tenth month, or December, was the last."

"That is so."

"Well, Numa, tell the Romans to reckon this

way: First month, January; second, February; third, March; fourth, April; fifth, May; sixth, June; then the seventh and eighth; ninth, September; tenth, October; eleventh, November; and last, December."

"All this I will explain to the people of Rome."

"And now, Numa, go again to the Lady of Silence, and think of what I have told you. Farewell."

What I have related to you is only a myth or legend. Perhaps there never was such a man as King Numa, although tradition calls him the second King of Rome, 715–672 B.C., and certainly there never was such a nymph as Egeria, the Lady of the Fountain in the Forest. But for many, many years the Romans believed that Numa was a King of Rome in very early times, and that he had learned wisdom from a nymph by the fountain. It does, indeed, need wisdom to govern cities and countries, for men have strong wills and are hard to rule. You know that persons who study how to rule are called politicians, and the rulers are called statesmen. The Romans were a great and wise people in many ways, and we may learn lessons from the history of their city and republic. Statesmen learn their business by reading history, and by listening to the words of other sage men, and by altering old laws and customs that are not now useful, and making new ones. We should respect the names of good statesmen, such as Pericles, the Greek; Cæsar, the Roman; William the Silent, the Dutchman; Oliver Cromwell, the Englishman; George Washington and Abraham Lincoln.

WHY THE ROMANS BORE PAIN

A ROMAN slave went into a dark room in search of something that was needed by his master. The room was a place for lumber. Pieces of old furniture stood here and there.

The slave was about to leave the chamber when he heard soft footsteps and voices that whispered. A group of young men, whom he could only just see in the dim light, entered the room, looking behind them as if to make sure that no eye saw them.

"No one will see us here," said one of the young men.

The slave hid himself at the back of a large chest. He held his breath as he peeped at the men and watched their deeds.

"Have you brought the blood?" asked one voice. "It is here in a cup," replied another.

"Are we all here?"

"We are—Titus, the son of Brutus; Tiberius, his brother; and the rest."

"We are all ready to fight for Tarquin?"

"Yes, yes!"

15

"He is our rightful king, and we want him back in Rome."

"Yes."

"The hard-hearted consul, Brutus, must be slain!"

"He must."

"Even though he is father to our friends here— Titus and Tiberius?"

"Yes."

"We will loyally stand by one another in this noble work for the sake of Rome."

"We will."

"Shall we all drink?"

"Yes."

The slave behind the chest shook with horror. He saw the young men, one by one, sip the red liquor in the cup. By this sign they swore to be true to one another in the plot against the life of Brutus. This was about 510 B.C.

"We will write letters to Tarquin the King," said one, as he wiped his lips. "We will tell him that we mean to kill Brutus and the other consul, and that soon we shall expect to see him in the city to rule over us once more as king."

The letter was written on a scrap of sheepskin, and folded up.

"You, sir," said one of the plotters to a person at his side, "are a friend of Tarquin. You will take him this letter."

"I will do so. I am staying at the house of the Aquilii, and in a few hours I shall leave the city, and take this joyful message to my lord."

"Let us go."

They all went quietly away, like thieves escaping from a back door.

The slave came from his hiding-place, and said to himself:

"What shall I do? The consuls are in danger. How dare I tell the father, Brutus, that his sons think to kill him? It is dreadful. But if I do nothing our consuls will die, and the city will fall into the hands of the bad King Tarquin, whose conduct has caused the Romans to hate him."

He made up his mind to go to Valerius, a very just and honest citizen, and to him he told all that he had heard and seen.

"Stay here in this room," said Valerius, "till I send for you. I shall run to the house of the Aquilii, and see if the letter is there."

To his wife he said: "Watch the door of the room. This slave must not stir from here till I return."

He ran off with a crowd of his friends and slaves, all carrying weapons. They came to the house of the Aquilii, forced their way in, searched the place from top to bottom, and found the letter. Just then a noise was heard at the gate of the house. A number of the plotters had taken the alarm, and they had hurried to seize the terrible letter of death. It was too late. They were captured, and taken off to the meeting-place of the senate—an open space surrounded by pillars. It was called the "Forum." The two consuls were fetched from their homes. They took their seats in the forum. Near them stood the lictors, bearing each a bundle of rods, with an axe tied to the bundle. Many senators sat in the hall also, and a crowd of Romans gathered round. The sky overhead was calm and blue, but the hearts of the plotters were moved with fear.

The slave was brought forward. He told his tale. The letter was produced, and was read out aloud. It was clear that these young men were traitors to the city of Rome, and false to its liberty. The worst plotters were Titus and Tiberius, the sons of the consul who sat in the forum.

For a short time there was a deep silence. The consul who sat next to Brutus had tears in his eyes—to think that his friend Brutus should have such sons! What would Brutus do?

"He had better send his sons to a far country," whispered a man in the crowd; and those who stood about murmured: "Yes; that would be better than sending his own children to death."

Then Brutus looked sternly at his sons, and spoke:

"You, Titus, and you, Tiberius, why do you not make your defence against the charge?"

No answer.

"You, Titus, and you, Tiberius, why do you not make your defence against the charge?"

No answer.

"You, Titus, and you, Tiberius, why do you not make your defence against the charge?"

To this third question, no answer.

Brutus turned to the officers.

"Lictors," he said, "the rest of the business is left to you."

Then the lictors laid hold of the youths, and stripped off their coats, and tied their hands behind them, and placed them on the ground, and flogged them with the rods.

Brutus said nothing. He looked neither to the right hand nor to the left.

At last the lictors took their axes, and cut off the heads of the sons of Brutus.

Then the father who had lost his sons rose up amid a great silence of the people, and went to his house.

"Oh," cried some, "how cruel a man is Brutus, to condemn his own sons to death!"

"Nay," said others, "he loved them all the time as his sons; but he is Consul of Rome, and it was his duty to defend Rome against her enemies."

The rest of the traitors were put to death, and

the freedom of the city was given to the slave. Henceforward he was a Roman citizen, and not a bondsman. He was the first slave in Rome to be enfranchised, or made free. The suffrage also was allowed to him; that is, he was able to vote at meetings, the same as other Romans.

Who can tell the pain that Brutus bore when he saw his own sons die? Why did he bear this pain? Because he loved justice more than he loved his own flesh and blood.

I will tell you of another Roman who lived at the same time, and who bore pain for the sake of the city of Rome, though it was pain of another kind.

Tarquin, the king, who is believed to have reigned from 534–510 B.C., had a friend named Porsenna, who was king of the Etruscan people. Porsenna laid siege to the city of Rome. The Romans were in deep distress. Food ran short, and the foes without the gates were strong.

One day King Porsenna sat in his camp with his nobles about him. They were talking of the best manner in which to attack the city. From the camp they could see the river Tiber, and the wooden bridge over the yellow stream, and the high walls of Rome, and the roof of the temple, and the hill of the Capitol.

A shout was heard. One of the king's officers had been struck down by a stranger with a sword. A scuffle took place. The stranger was seized, and brought before the king. The sword had been snatched from his hand.

A small bronze altar stood near the king. On the top of the altar flickered a fire, in which the king was going to burn a sacrifice to the gods of the Etruscan people.

"Who are you?" asked the king of the stranger.

"I am a Roman."

"What is your name?"

"Mutius."

"Why did you kill my officer?"

"I thought it was you, sir. I meant to kill you."

As he spoke Mutius held out his right hand and thrust it into the flames of the fire on the altar. The flesh of his hand was scorched, but he did not flinch. He gazed steadily into the face of the king.

"Take your hand away from the fire!" cried the king. "Brave man, here is your sword."

Mutius took the sword in his left hand, and his right hand dropped at his side. He would never again have the proper use of his right hand.

"King," he said, "you see we Romans do not fear pain when we do service to our city. For the sake of Rome we are ready to sacrifice our hands, our hearts, our lives. I am not the only one who is willing to suffer. There are in the city three hundred young men who have sworn to slay you if I did not succeed. At any moment any of them may fall upon you and rob the Etruscans of their king."

The king admired the valor of Mutius and the

spirit of the Roman people. He let him go free, and made peace with the city of Rome, and retired to his own country.

Brutus, for the sake of justice and of the city of Rome, bore pain in his heart and soul. Mutius, for the sake of Rome, bore pain in his body. Neither of them thought of his own comfort. Each of them lived for others.

THE SECOND FOUNDER
OF ROME

THE general of the Roman army stood on a high tower, and looked over the walls. Thence he saw the streets of a city. Men ran up and down the streets with shouts. Houses blazed with fire. Roman soldiers were carrying bundles of spoil. The city had belonged to the Etruscan people, and had fallen into the hands of the Romans after a siege of ten years.

"This is a grand success, sir," said some of the general's friends.

Then the general, whose name was Camillus, lifted up his hands toward heaven and spoke this prayer: "If, O ye gods, you think Rome must not have too much glory; and if you think that, after this victory, we must suffer some trouble to keep us from being too proud, oh, I pray you, let the trouble fall, not upon Rome, but upon me."

Thus did Camillus love his country more than he loved himself.

He laid siege to another town. The huts of his army were built in a ring about the fortress, but between the Roman camp and the city walls was an open space of meadows. A schoolmaster now and then brought his boys out of the city and let them play in this open space. At first they sported near the walls. Little by little he drew them nearer the Roman camp. One day he led his troop of lads to the guards of the camp and said:

"I surrender to you, and also place these boys in your charge."

The schoolmaster and his scholars were led before Camillus. He expected the Roman general to be greatly pleased at getting the sons of so many of the besieged citizens into his hands. But Camillus had no such thoughts. He looked sternly upon the traitor, and said:

"War is a savage thing, and many cruel acts are done in war. But there are laws even in war, and men of honor will obey those laws. Surely it would be dishonorable of me to make captives of these boys whom you have brought to my camp by a mean trick."

He turned to the lictors, and bade them seize the schoolmaster. They tied his hands behind him, and gave rods to the lads.

"Boys," said Camillus, "drive him back to the city. He is a traitor."

Fathers and mothers and friends had gathered on the walls, in great grief for the loss of the boys. Presently, to their surprise, they beheld the lads returning, and the biggest scholars were laying the rods smartly upon the traitor's back.

Soon afterward the city yielded to the Romans.

Camillus was a man of the upper or richer classes. The poorer classes, or plebeians (*ple-bee-ans*), often quarrelled with their richer neighbors; and I am sorry to say the quarrel of the rich and poor lasts even to our own day. Camillus, quiet as he was, was obliged to fly from Rome because his deeds and his ideas did not please the mass of the people. As he left the city he paused, looked back at its walls and towers, and stretched out his hands and said:

"Through no fault of mine, I am forced to leave Rome. Some day Rome will regret having driven me out."

Much trouble then happened to the Romans and to Italy. The Gauls from the north had crossed the rock and snows of the Alps, and entered the fruitful land of Italy. Their numbers were large, their shields and helmets glittered with a brightness that made them terrible. The Romans lost a battle, and their city was in danger. The fire-maidens carried the burning coals in a vessel, snatched up the images of the gods, and fled from Rome. Crowds of city folk were hurrying away, some carrying furniture on their backs, some riding on horses or in wagons. One good Roman, who was escaping with his wife and children, saw the vestal virgins (or fire-maidens) wearily trudging along by the river Tiber. He invited them to ride in his wagon, and they were glad to accept his aid.

The third day after the battle the Gauls arrived at Rome, and saw the gates open, and the streets deserted by the people. Brennus, their captain, led his men into the city. At length they came to the forum.

There sat the elders or senators, and all sat silent. They would not leave Rome in the hour of need.

The Gauls crowded round, and gazed in wonder at the old rulers. At last one of them went forward and touched the beard of one of the senators. The bearded Roman struck the Gaul with his staff and wounded him. The Gaul slew the senator with his sword. Then the rest of the elders were slain. Think of these noble Romans lying dead on the floor of the forum! They were faithful to the end.

Camillus stayed in the country some distance from Rome. He had felt bitter against the city which he had loved, and still loved in the bottom of his heart. One day he led some of the people out of a small town toward a camp where a party of Gauls were intrenched. At midnight the trumpets sounded. Camillus and his followers fell upon the camp and gained a victory.

When this news came to the ears of the Romans who had fled from Rome, many of them held a meeting and sent a messenger to beg him to take the lead once more.

"I will come," said he, "if I am invited by the people in the Capitol."

Ah, the Capitol was a hill inside the walls of Rome, and on it stood a fortress, and in this fortress was a body of citizens who would not yield to Brennus and his Gauls. But how was word to be carried to the Capitol? Who would go?

A young man dressed himself in rough clothes, so as to appear like a common peasant, and he hid large pieces of cork under his clothes. Having travelled to the river Tiber, which runs by Rome, he made his garments into a bundle and placed the bundle on his head and fastened the corks together for a float, and as he held the float he swam across the river by night. Then he crept through back streets till he came to the Capitol. Up the rugged cliff he climbed in the darkness, and gained the top in safety. Some senators were among the garrison of the Capitol. They heard the young man's story.

"Go," they said, "and bid Camillus march to the help of Rome."

The young hero climbed down the cliff again, crossed the river unseen, and gave the order to Camillus.

But before Camillus could rescue Rome the Gauls tried to seize the Capitol. One night they began to scale the cliff as the young messenger had done. A few of them actually reached the top, and others were climbing behind. The Roman guards were asleep.

A temple of Juno, the goddess, stood on the Capitol. In this building were kept a flock of geese. The birds heard the slight noise made by the Gauls, and they hissed! The sound woke the Romans. All was alarm! The clash of spears and shields resounded. The Gauls were driven back, some being flung headlong down the precipice. Ever afterward the story ran that Juno's geese had saved the Capitol.

Camillus had not come yet. The hearts of the Romans were faint. Food was almost gone. At length they sent to Brennus.

"Will you retire from the city if we give you a thousand pounds' weight of gold?"

"I will."

Scales were brought to weigh the gold. Shining pieces were piled up in one scale so as to balance the weights on the other. One of the Gauls held down the scale that contained the weights.

"You are unjust!" cried the Roman.

Brennus laughed. He threw his belt and the sword tied to it into the scale, making it drop lower.

"Woe to the conquered!" he cried.

The Romans were obliged to pile up more gold, so as to balance the extra weight of the captain's belt and sword.

The Gauls did at last leave the Romans in peace, though I am not sure if they were driven out by Camillus, or went because they loved their own land better. You see, the Romans had been beaten by the Gauls, and felt too proud to own their defeat, and the writers of old histories do not tell us very clearly what happened at this time.

As I told you, Camillus belonged to the upper class, or richer class, who were called "patricians." Quarrels still went on between the people of wealth and the people who were poor, and at one time a number of the poorer citizens threatened to leave

Rome altogether and set up a city somewhere else. They said that it was not right that the two magistrates who were chosen to govern Rome every year should always be men of the upper class. One ought to be a commoner, or plebeian. Camillus thought it was wise to grant this, and each year one consul was elected by the votes of the patricians and one by the votes of the commoners. This is what happens in politics. One class want one thing, and one class want another; and the wisest heads among the people have to plan a way to please as many of the citizens as possible. When the city was at peace again, the people built a new temple, called the temple of Concord, or Friendship. It stood by the forum. I wish such a temple could be built in every city and every land, and that the hearts of all men were joined together in peace and goodwill. And because Camillus made the city strong again after all its troubles with the Gauls and the quarrels of the citizens, the people called him "the second founder of Rome." He died 365 B.C.

THE MAN WHO WAITED

"HAVE you heard that drops of blood came out on the shields of the soldiers?"

"Indeed! And in the corn-fields, so I am told, corn has been cut that ran with blood!"

"Yes, neighbors, and I hear that red-hot stones have been seen to fall from the air!"

"These things are terrible! What do they mean?"

"I fear that the Romans will be beaten by the foe from Africa. This man Hannibal is a mighty man of war. He has crossed the Alps; he has marched through Tuscany; nothing seems to stay his course."

So talked a group of people in Rome. Not long afterward a battle was fought, and it is said that fifteen thousand Romans were slain by Hannibal's army, and as many again were taken prisoners.

The awful tidings came to Rome. A magistrate called the people together, and said:

"Romans! we have lost a great battle. Our army is cut to pieces. The consul is killed. Think, therefore, what is to be done to save Rome."

A sad murmur was heard through the vast crowd. Then voices were heard:

"Fabius! Let Fabius lead us! Let Fabius be made dictator! Fabius shall be our war-lord!"

So Fabius was chosen general of a new Roman army. Do you suppose he went all at once to attack Hannibal? No. He was a man who was willing to wait. Hannibal was too strong to be beaten yet. Fabius kept his troops on the hills, always watching the enemy in the valleys, but not coming down in full force. Now and then a body of the Romans would rush down a mountain-side and seize Hannibal's cattle, or slay some of his soldiers, and then quickly return to the rocky heights. By this means Fabius thought he should wear the enemy out.

Some of the Romans did not like this slow style of war. A captain named Minucius said, with a sneer:

"Well, I wonder whether Fabius means to carry the army up to the sky, as he is so fond of camping on the hilltops."

Hannibal's host nearly got caught once. They found themselves among the mountains. The only road out was narrow, and it was blocked by four thousand men from the army of Fabius. Night was coming on, and fear took hold of the men of Carthage (for Hannibal came from Carthage in Africa). Their leader did not fear. He told his men to tie bunches of dry bushwood to the horns of two thousand cattle, and set light to the torches, and drive the oxen forward. This was done. In the darkness of the night the Romans

31

saw the strange lights dancing and flashing in the valley, and supposed a mass of the enemy were approaching, and they fled up the hills. Then Hannibal hastily pressed on with his army, and escaped into a more open country.

Fabius followed slowly, as before. He had exchanged prisoners with Hannibal—that is, for every hundred prisoners given up by the Romans a hundred were given up by Hannibal. But two hundred and forty Romans were still left in the camp of the African. The senate at Rome would not send Fabius the money to buy these prisoners off. Fabius had compassion on his captive countrymen. He sent his son to Rome to sell some of his land. With the money thus gained, Fabius redeemed the rest of the prisoners. Thus he helped his fellow-soldiers at his own cost. Some of them offered to pay him back their ransom, but he would take nothing.

At length the senate of Rome elected Minucius as a second general. They thought he would act more rapidly, and win battles sooner. Fabius did not think it wise for two generals to lead one army; so he divided the Roman host, and each part encamped in a separate spot. The sharp-eyed Hannibal noted all that went on. He decided to fight Minucius. He placed a number of his men in hiding in ditches and hollows around about a hill. A small body of his army appeared on a low hill. Minucius saw them.

"Oh," he said to his captains, "we can easily drive Hannibal's troops from that hill."

The Romans hurried to the attack. From many a ditch and hollow the Africans rose up with a shout, and soon the legions of Minucius were flying in disorder.

From his camp Fabius had watched these events. He slapped his hand upon his thigh in token of grief, and said:

"How soon has Minucius done what I feared he would! He acted rashly, and punished himself."

Fabius then moved his part of the army to the aid of his comrade, and checked the advance of Hannibal.

After the battle Minucius called his men round him, and thus addressed them:

"Friends and fellow-soldiers: Every man makes mistakes; and when a mistake is made, we should do our best to correct it. I have been in the wrong in not following the advice of Fabius. Come with me, and I will tell him there shall be but one army, and he shall be the one leader."

The ensigns who carried the wooden eagles then advanced, and Minucius came after them with all his troops. He visited Fabius in his tent. They talked together a few minutes, and came out. Then Minucius spoke with a loud voice:

"Father!"

As he said this he bowed to Fabius. Then the soldiers of Minucius shouted:

"Patrons!"

As they cried "patrons" (which means friends and masters) they saluted the soldiers of Fabius. Then Minucius said:

"Fabius, you have to-day gained two victories—one over the enemy from Africa by your courage, the other over me by your prudence and kindness, for to you we owe our lives. And I call you 'father,' since I know no better name."

So saying, he embraced Fabius, and the two divisions of the army came together in friendship. Thus did Romans know how to keep down jealous feelings for the sake of Rome.

Alas! more sufferings were to be borne by Rome. In the battle of Cannæ about fifty thousand Romans fell. At the close of this awful scene Hannibal's friends gathered round him.

"Go on, general!" they cried. "In five days you will reach Rome, and eat supper on the Capitol."

Hannibal did not take their advice.

Meanwhile the consul Varro, who had commanded the defeated army, had come to the city. The whole senate and people went to meet him at the gate. Varro looked sad and grave, but he did not tremble as a coward.

"Romans," he said, "all is not lost, in spite of so many having died. I have returned to do what I can to help the city."

Fabius was among the crowd. And he and the other rulers said:

"Varro, we praise you because you do not despair of the fortunes of Rome."

No, whatever happened, the people of this proud city did not altogether lose heart. And much of their confidence was due to Fabius. He was seen in the streets, walking in a quiet and easy manner as if nothing dreadful had happened. His face was calm, his voice had no trembling in it. At the gates he placed guards who should prevent citizens from fleeing away in sudden panic. When he took the field again he kept up the same tactics (or plan) by avoiding any big battle and hanging at the rear and sides of Hannibal's army. And he succeeded in winning back several strong cities that had been captured by the Africans.

When Fabius was old he was pleased at his son being chosen consul.

One day the consul was at a public assembly. Old Fabius, riding on a horse, came near to speak to his son. But, according to the laws of Rome, no mounted men might come near a consul. When the consul saw his father on horseback, he called to him one of his lictors. You remember, a lictor was an officer who carried a bundle of rods and an axe.

"Lictor," he said, "bid Fabius dismount and come on foot to me if he has any business with me."

The lictor did as he was ordered. Silence fell upon the people. They looked angrily at the consul; they looked with pity at the old general.

"How wrong," they said, "for a son to treat a father with such disrespect. And Fabius has spent his life in the service of Rome."

But Fabius did not think as they did. He alighted from his horse at once, and hastened to his son, and put his arms about him.

"My son," he said, "I am glad you understand your office. It is in this way that we and our forefathers have made Rome a great city. We have not sought to put our own feelings first. We have placed the honor of Rome above our love for father or son."

Fabius died in the year 203 B.C. He had been five times consul; and twice he had ridden through the streets of Rome in a triumph or procession of joy after victory. He died poor. You remember how he paid out of his own purse the ransoms of many Roman prisoners. The people of Rome resolved that he should be buried in a way that showed how much they loved his memory. Every citizen gave a small piece of money toward the expenses of the funeral.

HOW A WOMAN SAVED ROME

"COMRADES, let us leave the city!"

"We will go at once!"

"There is plenty of air and water in Italy. We have no need to stay in Rome!"

"And we can die and be buried outside Rome!"

"Forward!"

And so the common folk, or plebeians, of Rome shouted to one another as they marched through the streets with their wives and children. They thought they were wrongly treated by the richer people, who were called patricians. They did the hard work of Rome—hewed the wood, drew the water, built the houses, tilled the land; and yet they were not allowed their fair share of the government of the city.

The old men of the senate were alarmed.

"We cannot do without the working-men," they said. "We must fetch them back, or else they will found a new city."

Several senators were chosen to follow after the plebeians, and persuade them to come back. The chief among these messengers was Agrippa, and he spoke very earnestly to the people:

"Friends, Romans, countrymen: The senate desires you to return. You shall be justly treated. You shall elect some of your number to sit with the senators. We need you, and you need us."

"Ah, but do we need you patricians?" murmured the people.

"Let me tell you a fable, Romans. Once there was a man whose legs, arms, fingers, feet, and mouth made a great rebellion against his stomach. They said the stomach did nothing, while the mouth talked, the legs walked, the arms pulled, the fingers worked, the feet stamped. So the stomach refused to do anything, as they accused it of being idle. Then the body of this man pined away till it was mere skin and bone. All the parts of the body, Romans, need one another. The patricians need you working-men, and you need the patricians to lead you and advise you, in peace and war. Come back to Rome, and we will agree that you shall choose five people's men, or tribunes, who shall sit with the senate, and take a share in the ruling of the city."

The plebeians went back, and the five tribunes had seats at the door of the senate hall. Whenever the senators made a law that seemed unjust to the people, the tribunes rose from their seats and cried aloud:

"Veto!"

This word means, "I forbid."

Among the patricians at this time was a man of noble spirit named Marcius. Very brave was his conduct at the siege of Corioli, the capital of the Volscian country. He was in the thick of the fight, and was covered with blood and sweat. The soldiers agreed to give him a new name after the town which he took, and therefore he was called Coriolanus. Much plunder was captured—gold, silver, etc. The plunder was piled in a heap before the army, and the consul of Rome told Coriolanus that he might have a beautiful horse for himself, and also a tenth part of the spoil.

"No," said he, "I will indeed accept the horse, but let the spoil be divided among the men, and I will take my share—nothing more—the same as the rest. But I will ask for one favor, sir."

"What is that?"

"Among the Volscian prisoners is a friend of mine, who will, in the usual course, be sold as a slave. Grant me his freedom, for he has been kind to me, and is a man of virtue."

All the army praised his goodness of heart, and the consul granted his desire.

For seventeen years Coriolanus, who lived in the first half of the fifth century B.C., served the city in war and in the work of governing, and at last he was made consul. But then came troubles. He had never liked the tribunes. He thought too much had been given to the common people. In his ideas he was an aristocrat—that is, he thought the superior class of men should hold the sway over the less worthy and

39

more ignorant class. But then, you see, the plebeians would not consider themselves less worthy or more ignorant. When a large stock of corn was brought into Rome, as a present from the King of Syracuse, the people saw the loaded wagons and mules, and hoped that they might all receive shares of it gratis, or free.

"No," said the consul to the senate, "we must not yield to the people, and flatter them, and give them all they demand. If we do so, there will be no end to their requests, and the city will be filled with disorder."

The tribunes, hearing this, ran into the streets, and called the citizens together. The senate broke up in confusion.

Next morning the senators met again in the forum, and talked of the best way to deal with the corn. Some wished to sell it cheap to the people. Coriolanus said "No," and he defied the people in angry words and with haughty looks.

"He shall die!" shouted the tribunes.

They were about to carry him to the top of the Tarpeian rock, and hurl him down the precipice. His friends defended him. At length it was agreed that he should stand trial in a great assembly of the Romans on a certain market-day. The trial was held. The majority of votes were against him. What should be his punishment? Banishment for life. Never must he set foot in Rome again. His friends were deeply grieved. He alone kept a cool mind and a face unmoved. First, he went to his house and kissed his mother and wife. Then, amid a crowd of patricians, he walked firmly to one of the city gates, and there they bade him goodbye. With three or four companions he travelled into the country, staying at farm-houses. Then he went on alone.

He had dressed himself in mean garments like a rustic laborer. Where was he going? He had made up his mind to join the enemies of Rome—the very Volscians against whom he had so boldly fought.

One evening he reached the town of Antium, and walked through the streets. No one knew him. He stopped at the door of Tullus, a nobleman. Having entered, he sat down by the fire-side, close to the shelf where stood the little images of the household gods. Whoever sat by the household gods was looked upon as under their care; he must not be hurt. The people of the house were much surprised at the stranger's entrance. They hurried into the room where Tullus sat at supper, and told him.

"Who are you?" asked Tullus. "And what is your business here?"

The Roman drew the cloak away from his face, and said:

"Do you not know me, Tullus? I am he who was the foe of the Volscians. The city which I captured gave me my name, Coriolanus. But I have received an evil reward for all my service. The mob of common people insulted me. The patricians were too cowardly to assist me. I mean to take my revenge on Rome. I have come to join the Volscians. I shall fight much better for you than I have fought against you."

"Welcome," cried Tullus. "We shall be glad of

your friendship, and grateful for your aid in the war against Rome."

They sat down to table, and talked long and earnestly on the best modes of carrying on the struggle.

One day Tullus called a meeting of the Volscians, and told them of the new ally, or comrade, who had come from Rome. Coriolanus then appeared before the people and addressed them. They were charmed by his speech, and declared themselves ready to follow him anywhere.

With the Volscian troops he marched toward his native city, setting fire to farm-houses and villages, and capturing fortresses, and beating back bodies of Romans who were sent out to check his progress. The city was in alarm. Women ran up and down the streets, and old men knelt praying before the altars of the gods.

Some of the senators, who had once been friends of Coriolanus, offered to go and confer with him in his camp.

"I will make peace," he replied to these messengers, "if the Romans give back all the land they have taken from the Volscians. You may have thirty days to think about it."

They returned to his camp in thirty days, and said the Romans would yield a part of the land if the Volscians would lay down their arms.

"No," he answered, "and you can now have but three more days before I resume the war."

A third party came. This consisted of priests bearing their wands and staves. To these he spoke as sternly as to the senators.

A wise lady named Valeria thought of a plan. She took a number of Roman matrons with her, and they called at the house where lived Volumnia, the aged mother of Coriolanus. They found her sitting with her daughter-in-law, the wife of Coriolanus; and his children were with the mother and grandmother.

"We come to you," said the visitors, "as women to women, not being sent by the senate or the consuls. We come to beg your help. Go along with us to Coriolanus. Tell him that, though you are his mother, the Romans have done you no harm, in spite of his joining the enemies of our city. You will bring him to a better mind."

To this Volumnia agreed. She took with her her daughter-in-law and the children, and a number of the Roman ladies accompanied her to the camp. The general sat in his chair of state, and when he saw a party approaching he at first supposed it must be the senators. As they drew nearer, to his surprise he beheld women. He saw his mother, his wife, his children. Rising from his chair, he ran to meet them and kiss them, and the tears fell from his eyes.

"My son," then said his mother, "you see how unhappy we all appear. The women in Rome are also unhappy. How else should we feel when we see a Roman encamped against Rome? A battle will be fought. Whoever wins, we shall be miserable. Your wife will see Rome beaten, or you. If you win, and if you march into Rome as a victor, you shall pass over the dead body of your mother; for I will not live to see Rome conquered by my son. Make peace, I beg of you. The Volscians are strong, and it will be to their honor to make peace; and Rome will thank you. Your mother has done much for you. What have you done for her?"

So saying, the old matron knelt at his feet, as did also his wife and children.

"Oh, mother!" cried Coriolanus, as he raised her up, "what have you done? You have gained a victory, and saved Rome, but ruined me."

He sent the women back to Rome, and the next morning he drew off the army and marched it back to the Volscian country. The Volscians let him do so, for they felt that only Coriolanus was able enough a leader to conduct the war against Rome. Without him there could be little worth doing. The Romans rejoiced, and the citizens crowded to the temples to place garlands of flowers on the altars of the gods. All the men praised the work of the women who had gone with such courage to the camp and prayed for mercy.

The elders of the senate met, and made a decree that the women might have whatever reward they chose.

"We desire only one thing," said the Roman ladies. "Let a new temple be built for the Good-Fortune of Women. We will subscribe the money for the building."

The senate said the temple should be set up at the public expense.

Nevertheless, the Roman ladies each paid what they were able to the fund; and when the temple was built, about four miles outside the city, on the spot where the tent of Coriolanus had rested, the first priestess to take charge of it was the aged mother who had saved Rome.

Not long afterward Coriolanus was killed by the daggers of the Volscians, who were angry because he had spared Rome.

I am not sure what you will think of the conduct of Coriolanus. But I am sure you will admire the action of Volumnia and the matrons. And you girls who read this story will, I hope, see that you have a part to play for your city and your country.

THE TRIUMPH

"WHY do you weep, my child?" asked a Roman father of his little girl, as he took her in his arms.

"P—P—Per—Perseus is dead!" she sobbed.

"Which Perseus do you mean?"

"The dear little dog, father."

Ah, the dear little dog. But Perseus was the name of the King of Macedonia also, and it was of this Perseus that the Roman father was thinking.

This father was the general Lucius Æmilius Paulus, afterward surnamed Macedonicus, who had fought for Rome during many years. In Spain he had placed the Roman eagle over two hundred and fifty cities. He lived from about 229–160 B.C.

King Perseus expected the coming of the Romans. He had collected an army of his people, and hoped to add more warriors by hiring fighting-men from the banks of the river Danube. Ten thousand horsemen, each with a footman running at his side, arrived at the camp of Perseus, offering to fight for pay. The horsemen were tall, brawny fellows, and ready to give battle to anybody on earth. But their price was high. Each officer from the Danube land demanded one thousand pieces of gold.

Perseus was very fond of money. He often counted his gold, and he sealed it up in bags.

"No," he said to the barbarian horsemen, "I will not pay the sum you ask. It is too dear."

And the ten thousand cavalry rode back to the Danube, and left the King of Macedonia to meet the Romans as best he could.

Æmilius Paulus had pitched his camp one night, and the Roman army had had supper. The moon was shining at the full. Presently a shadow began to glide slowly over the face of the moon, and, after a while, all its surface was covered with a reddish-gray tint. It was an eclipse, caused by the shadow of the earth being thrown upon the moon. Paulus had known it was coming—an astronomer had told him. And Paulus too warned his army, lest they should be alarmed. The Romans made a great noise by striking brass pans, and they waved lighted torches; for they always acted so, after the manner of their forefathers, when an eclipse took place. The Macedonians were silent and sad.

"This shadow on the moon," they whispered, "foretells the fall of our king."

When the moon was shining again as usual, Paulus had eleven young cows slain and burned as an offering to the gods.

The next day the battle joined. Perseus watched his warriors go forward to meet the Romans. The tall men of Thrace had white shields, black jackets, long pikes. Persians also were among the hired fighters. The young men of Macedon had purple coats, their armor and weapons were glittering, their shields were brass. You have heard of the phalanx (*fal-anks*)—how the men of Macedon held their shields close together, so as to form a wall of brass; and over this wall they thrust their long spears. Enemies would charge wildly against the phalanx, but could seldom break through this living and moving fortress. The Romans were not cowed by the phalanx. At three in the afternoon they made the attack, and by sunset the victory was won, and Paulus returned to his tent, which had been covered with ivy and laurel leaves in token of success.

Perseus fled with the horsemen. The foot-soldiers came up with them, and called them cowards, and pulled some from their steeds. The king feared lest he should be treated likewise. He turned his horse off the highroad, rolled up his purple cloak, placed it in a bundle on his saddle, and galloped away wildly. A few friends went with him. None of them felt respect for this timid prince. One stopped to tie his shoe, another to give drink to a horse, a third to take a draught of water himself. One by one they all left him, except a small body-guard of Cretans (men from the Island of Crete), and they only followed him for pay. Perseus had a large treasure with him; and, in terror lest the Cretans should forsake him, he gave them several gold and silver cups. When he reached a place of safety he actually went to the Cretans, and, with tears in his eyes, begged them to return the cups, for which he promised to pay!

The Romans scoured the land in search of the flying king. Perseus took ship, and sailed to an island in the Grecian sea. The Roman galleys pursued him even there. He bargained with a Crete sailor to carry him, his wife, and children, and treasure, in a ship to another land. The Cretan took the gold and silver, but said to Perseus:

"It will not be safe for you to sail by day. My boat will pass the Roman fleet. The Romans will see only me in it, and will not suspect me. Meet me at yonder point to-night, and I will take you and your family on board."

At the time fixed Perseus was there. The Cretan was not there. A passing islander told him the ship had set sail some hours before. In a few days he was a prisoner in the hands of the Romans, and was brought to the general.

Paulus rose from his seat to meet him. Perseus flung himself on the ground, and caught hold, as a slave might, of the general's knees.

"Oh, sir," he groaned, "show mercy on me; oh, show mercy on me, poor wretch that I am!"

"Wretch, indeed," answered Paulus, "to behave thus. We Romans always respect a foe who is brave, and we feel contempt for cowards."

Paulus then conquered Macedonia. Sometimes his soldiers broke loose, and ran riot in the Greek cities, robbing and plundering. But, so far as he was able, the general kept his army in discipline, and he behaved kindly and humanely to the conquered people. At last he sailed back to Rome, where the citizens were waiting to give him a welcome, or Triumph.

In the galley of Perseus the victor was rowed up the river Tiber. The galley was draped in cloth of scarlet and purple, and spears and bucklers taken from the foe shone brightly on its masts and deck. Multitudes of people stood on the river-banks shouting for joy.

On the first day of the welcoming of Æmilius Paulus platforms were set up in the streets of Rome for the people to stand on and watch the procession. The citizens were dressed in white. The gates of all the temples were open, and the temple walls were hung with garlands, and the priests burned sweet incense.

"Here they come!" cried the crowd.

First the lictors, each bearing a bundle of rods. They cleared the way for a long line of chariots, two hundred and fifty in number, conveying images, paintings, and large statues taken from the towns of Macedonia.

On the second day an immense number of wagons filed by, carrying helmets, shields, breastplates, bucklers, quivers full of arrows, swords, and pikes. After the wagons walked three thousand men in groups of four. Each group of four soldiers bore a box or some such vessel, filled with silver money. There were seven hundred and fifty of these vessels of coin. Other men had bowls, horns, goblets, cups—all of silver.

The last day was the chief day, and all the folk were early astir, clad again in white. Trumpeters sounded a charge. After them trudged one hundred and twenty fat oxen, their horns being gilded, and their necks gay with flowers. Boys followed with gold and silver vessels in their arms. Next appeared many men who brought seventy-seven chests full of gold coin. A chariot rolled by on which could be seen a man's armor in a heap. It had once belonged to King Perseus.

"Poor children," murmured the people, as they gazed at the next chariot.

In this car were the children of Perseus. They stretched out their hands toward the Roman crowd, begging for mercy. There were two boys and one girl, all young.

King Perseus walked behind this chariot. He was dressed in black, and his feet were shod with sandals. Behind him walked a troop of his courtiers, all looking miserable.

Last, the chariot of Paulus, drawn by four white horses, wreathed with garlands. His tunic was purple; his cloak purple, adorned with golden stars; his shoes gilded. An ivory sceptre was in his left hand, a branch of laurel in his right. A slave stood behind him, holding over his head the golden crown of Jupiter.

The Roman people shouted:

"Yo! yo! yo! Triumph! triumph! triumph! Yo! yo!"

But the slave, every now and then, whispered in the general's ear:

"Ah, but remember you are mortal! Remember

you will die!"

Thus the Romans taught themselves to be humble in the midst of their glory.

The soldiers of the army brought up the rear, singing lustily, and shouting, "Yo! Yo! Triumph!"

Alas! the general's heart was sorrowful. Five days before the Triumph his son, aged fourteen, had died.

And another grief was to come. Three days after the Triumph another son, aged twelve, also died.

At a meeting of the citizens Æmilius Paulus spoke.

"Friends," he said, "the winds of Fortune blow soft and fair, and sometimes they blow in dreadful tempest. In fifteen days I conquered Macedonia. I took much spoil, and had princes among my prisoners. Thus did Fortune blow fair. But two of my dear sons are now no more. I have buried them in the days of my triumph. The sons of Perseus, who was conquered, are still alive. The sons of Paulus, who conquered, are dead."

The people listened in deep silence, their hearts touched by the general's grief.

When Æmilius Paulus died the city greatly mourned. His bier (or funeral litter) was carried by young Macedonians and Spaniards. And some old Macedonians and Spaniards went behind, saying:

"He was good to us, even when he conquered us."

A ROMAN UNDISMAYED

TEN thousand Gauls, horsemen and footmen, waited on the plain for the onset of the Romans. The king was a very tall man. As he sat on his horse he seemed a giant. His armor, spangled with silver and gold, shone brightly in the sun. The Romans were led by the consul, Marcellus. They were advancing in a long, thin line.

The consul pressed his horse to a gallop, and pierced the breastplate of the Gaul with his spear. When he had slain the king, Marcellus leaped from his steed, took from the dead man some of his armor, and held it toward heaven, saying:

"O Jupiter, who seest how men bear themselves in battle, to thee I consecrate these spoils. Do thou grant us equal success in the rest of this war."

The armies then attacked each other, and the Romans won.

Not long afterward a terrible host of men from Africa—the men of Carthage, led by Hannibal—made its way through the passes of the Alps, and swept across North Italy toward Rome. It was sixteen years before the Romans defeated this general. At the battle of Cannæ the armies of Rome were beaten, and thousands of Romans fled to the city.

The elders of the senate resolved that these men who fled should not stay in Rome. They were all banished to the island of Sicily, with orders never to set foot on Italian soil again so long as Hannibal remained at war with Rome.

These Romans met Marcellus when he landed in Sicily with an army, on his way to the siege of Syracuse. That seaside town had taken sides against the Romans.

"Oh, sir," said the runaway Romans to the general, "we did indeed fly from the slaughter of Cannæ, but we still long to serve Rome, and we are ready to die for our fatherland. Take us into your service."

They knelt before him as they spoke.

Marcellus looked at them with pity. He was willing to try their courage. He had faith in them. So he wrote a letter to the senate at Rome, asking if he might add these men to his forces.

"Yes," replied the senate; "but however well they fight, you must give them no rewards."

They entered his army, and acted as brave men.

The siege of the large and beautiful city of Syracuse lasted about three years. Marcellus had a fleet in the harbor, as well as soldiers on land. The fleet consisted of sixty galleys, full of slings and stones, and other weapons of attack. Eight warships were fastened together so as to make a broad platform, on which were set up high scaling-ladders. As this vast engine reached the walls at the water-side, the Romans would climb up the ladders and leap on to the battlements of the walls.

The King of Syracuse saw with alarm the preparation of this machine. He called for his wisest man.

"My friend," he said, "you are the only man in Syracuse who can help me. Leave your drawings and your diagrams, your triangles, your cubes, your circles, your cones, your cylinders, your polygons, and all the rest. The city is in peril."

So the wisest man in the city busied himself for some days in ordering workmen to set up engines for slinging stones, and other objects of large size. These were not the only machines the engineer made, as you will see.

The Roman ships were rowed toward the town walls.

The engines began to act. Masses of stone and lumps of lead were hurled at the galleys of the besiegers, smashing the rigging and crushing the fighting-men and sailors.

Some of the Roman ships managed to reach the walls. Then huge beams of wood were lifted by machines, and their ends fell with tremendous force upon the galleys, beating down masts and men in their descent.

Other machines were yet more frightful. They thrust out enormous iron hooks over the walls, which gripped hold of a galley, lifted the ship half out of the water, and then quickly let it go, so that it heeled over and sank. The soldiers who tried to storm the walls on the land side of the city were baffled by engines of the same awful power. The Romans became at last so nervous that if they only saw a stick pushed over the top of the wall, they thought the mysterious engineer was about to work some mischief, and they retired in confusion.

Marcellus could not help smiling.

"This engineer," he said, "has a hundred hands."

The name of the clever engineer was Archimedes (*Ar-ki-mee-deez*). He was a great geometer—that is, he had a mighty mind for studying the measurements of things, and the forces by which they moved. Or, if you will pardon my using another long word, he was a great mathematician. Yet you see he did not keep his science for his own pleasure, in his own chamber, in his own house. He used his skill, or genius, to help his native country.

Marcellus, however, was undismayed. Never did he lose heart, no matter what dangers he had to withstand. He left off the attacks by sea and land. The city must be starved. After a long while the king sent word to ask Marcellus to parley, or treat, with him, and the Roman general went ashore to talk over terms of surrender. He went several times. Each time he took particular notice of a certain tower near the water, which he thought was easier to scale and capture than other towers of the city. One night, when the people in the city were drinking wine freely at the festival of the goddess Diana, the Romans climbed and captured the tower, and sounded their trumpets, and woke the whole city to surprise and terror. But months passed before the besiegers were able to take Syracuse from end to end. Then the city was sacked.

In the midst of the tumult a soldier ran into the house where Archimedes lived, and found the geometer tracing lines on the floor, and thinking deeply of some problem he was at work upon.

"Hold! hold!" cried the man of science, "don't disturb me. I am very much engaged!"

The soldier raised his sword and killed Archimedes. Marcellus was deeply grieved to hear of this deed.

After the taking of Syracuse, Marcellus again fought Hannibal in Italy. In one battle he was defeated. The Roman soldiers struggled back to their camp, dull and downcast. The general ordered that all the troops should be drawn up in array so that he might address them.

"I see before me," he said, sternly, "Roman arms and Roman bodies, but not one Roman man."

"General," called out one of the soldiers, "we regret that we fled."

"I will not pardon you," said he, "until you are victorious. To-morrow you will face the enemy again, and the news of your victory will reach Rome as soon as the news of your defeat."

Then, turning to the master of the stores, he added:

HANNIBAL & MARCELLUS

"Give these runaways barley."

So they had barley for supper, while the rest of the army had wheat.

Early next morning a red cloth was hung over the general's tent. That was the signal for battle. The men who ate barley took the front rank. That was where they wished to be posted.

Hannibal's elephants advanced in a terrible line. A Roman thrust his spear at one of these beasts. It retreated, and the rest of the elephants followed. The troops of Carthage were thrown into confusion. The Romans—barley first, wheat behind—charged with fury. Hannibal was beaten.

For the fifth time Marcellus was chosen consul of Rome. It was the last time; he was soon to die.

Very eagerly he sought to meet Hannibal again, to win one great and final victory. At length his scouts came in with the news that the general of Carthage was close at hand. The place was near Venusia.

Between the two armies was a hill, covered with copses and clumps of trees, and broken into hollows and rugged places. In these hollows Hannibal had concealed a good number of archers and spearmen. The Romans were anxious to seize this hill, as it overlooked the enemy's camp.

Marcellus, with his fellow-consul, his son, and two hundred and twenty horsemen, set out at a trot toward the hill. A sentinel had been posted on the hilltop to give warning. He saw Marcellus coming; he gave notice to his comrades. When the Romans were on the slope of the hill the men in ambush sprang out. Some of the Roman horsemen fled. Some closed round their general in a hand-to-hand fight. Both consuls were slain. This was in 208 B.C.

When the mighty captain of Carthage heard that Marcellus was dead he came to the fatal spot, and for a long time stood in silence, looking at the body of a man who was never dismayed. Being brave himself, he esteemed bravery in others. Presently he issued an order to his attendants.

"Let the body of Marcellus be dressed in rich robes, and then burned on a funeral pyre. Place the ashes in a silver urn. On the lid of the urn set a crown of gold, and carry it to his son. Marcellus was a noble Roman."

CATO THE STERN

A YOUNG fellow, seventeen years old, fought in the front ranks of the Roman army in the wars with Hannibal. His hair was red, his gray eyes flashed, his shout was a roar. Not a man in the host bore himself more boldly than young Cato.

After a battle he would retire to his tent; there he would help his slave prepare the supper of plain food. For drink he seldom had anything but water. If he was tired, he would have a dash of vinegar in the cup. Scarcely ever did he taste wine.

Cato became owner of an estate and a farmhouse. Near his own dwelling stood an old cottage, which the country-folk would point to, saying:

"This cottage once belonged to the consul who supped on turnips."

Yes, and this was the story. Manius Curius, the consul, was peeling turnips for his supper one evening as he sat in the chimney-corner A group of men entered in a quiet manner, as if not wishing to be heard by passers-by. They were messengers from the Samnite people, who were at war with Rome, and they brought Manius a large gift of gold in order to gain the favor of so valiant a foe.

"No," he said, "a man who can be satisfied with such a supper as this has no need of gold; and I think it more glorious to conquer the Samnites than to take their gold." The messengers went away looking foolish.

So Cato would look at the ancient cottage and say to himself:

"I should like to live as Manius lived, in a very simple style; and I should like to be a famous man in Rome, as he was."

His clothes were coarse. He worked with his slaves, ate the same kind of bread as they did, and drank the same kind of drink. Not only could he work; he could talk in a witty, sensible way, and when a neighbor went to law before a judge Cato would often speak on his behalf, so that, after a while, he went to act as a pleader, or speaker, in the law courts of Rome. People would repeat his shrewd sayings, such as:

"Wise men learn more from fools than fools from the wise; for the wise avoid the errors of fools, while fools do not profit by the examples of the wise."

And another:

"I do not like a soldier who moves his hands in marching and his feet in fighting, and who snores louder in bed than he shouts in battle."

Cato was chosen consul, and took command of an army in Spain, where he conquered four hundred cities. Also he waged war with the wild tribes on the banks of the river Danube. Also he fought the King of Syria, who had invaded Greece. In that country the mountains are many. The King of Syria occupied a pass among the hills, and had made his position strong by throwing up walls and mounds. Cato resolved to surprise the king's camp by night, and set out with a strong band of men, with one of his prisoners acting as guide. This guide missed the way. Cato and his companions wandered amid rocks and thickets. He ordered his men to wait while he and a friend climbed the rocky cliff, catching hold of wild olive-trees to help themselves up by; and presently they found a good path. They went down, called the soldiers to follow, and soon all were on the top of the hill. Then they came to a dead stop. A steep precipice fell away below their feet. A gray light began to glimmer in the eastern sky. Day was dawning. A hum of voices was heard below. Cato saw the king's camp some distance off, and the voices came from an advance-guard. Some of the Romans crept down the cliff and drove the guard off, all except one man, whom they brought to their captain. In answer to Cato's questions, he said the entrance to the pass was kept by only six hundred of the Syrian soldiers.

Sword in hand, Cato led the way, his trumpeters sounding the charge. The rest of the army broke into the camp at another point. A stone was flung which broke the king's teeth. The Syrian army hurried along a narrow road, one side of which was hemmed in by rocks, the other by muddy swamps, and many perished.

Cato was chosen censor by the citizens of Rome. It was his duty to watch the daily actions and manners of the people; and very strictly did he perform this duty. He made a list of the people who were extra rich in furniture and clothes, and he made them pay taxes at a higher rate than those less wealthy. When he found certain greedy citizens who watered their gardens with water which was only intended for public fountains, he cut the pipes. He offended the thieves, but he saved the public money. He disliked all vain show. He loved the ways of the Spartans, of which I have told you in the stories of the Greeks. He would allow no cruelty to pass unpunished, and he used to say that a man who beat his wife and children was cruel to the most sacred things in the world.

Cato would not let his son be taught by a slave, as other Roman fathers often did. He taught the boy himself, and gave him lessons in throwing a dart, riding, boxing, and swimming. Also, he taught him to write Latin in large, bold letters; and the boy wrote and learned tales of the old Roman heroes, such as I have related to you in these pages.

His wealth increased; he had more land, more slaves. So thrifty was he with his money that he saved enough to buy fish-ponds, hot baths, yards for fulling (or cleaning) cloth, and pasture, all of which he let for rents. He even lent money to his slaves, who bought boys in the slave-markets, and trained them to do various kinds of work and sold them at a profit to Cato. This will seem a wicked thing to you, but the Greeks, Romans, Hebrews, and other ancient nations kept slaves, and thought it no crime to do so; and in many cases the slaves were well treated.

As he was stern to the Roman citizens and to slaves, so he was stern to Rome's enemies. In his time Rome was still at war with Carthage, the famous city on the coast of Africa. Cato hated this city, and would finish his speeches in the forum by saying, "And Carthage must be destroyed," no matter what else he was talking about. Thus he might say:

"It is a good thing, O Romans, to teach our sons healthy exercises, to be hardy, to be thrifty, and to serve their fatherland even unto death. And Carthage must be destroyed!"

Or perhaps:

"He who takes what belongs to the public is a thief, even though he is a man of noble birth and dwells in a villa. And Carthage must be destroyed!"

And Carthage was indeed destroyed 146 B.C., but not till after Cato's death, which occurred 149 B.C.

I am sorry to tell you that, when any slave of his was old and useless, he would sell him. The writer Plutarch (*Ploo-tark*), in whose book I find the tales I tell you, was a kind-hearted man, and he made some wise remarks about justice to servants, and even animals that serve us; and I will copy his words out for you:

A good man will take care of his horses and dogs, not only while they are young, but when old and past service. Thus the people of Athens, when they had finished building a temple, set at liberty the beasts of burden that had been chiefly employed in that work, suffering them to pasture at large, free from any further service. It is said that one of them afterward came of its own accord to work, and, putting himself at the head of the laboring cattle, marched before them to the citadel. This pleased the people, and they made a decree that it should be kept at the public expense as long as it lived. The graves of Kimori's mares, with which he thrice won races at the Olympic games, are still to be seen near his own tomb. Many men have shown particular marks of regard in burying the dogs which they had cherished and been fond of. Among the rest was the dog who swam by the side of a galley at the battle of Salamis, and was afterward buried by his master upon a headland by the sea, the place being called "The Dog's Grave" to this day. We certainly ought not to treat living creatures like shoes or household goods which, when worn out with use, we throw away. And, if it were only to learn kindness to mankind, we should practise mercy to other creatures. For my own part, I would not sell even an old ox that had toiled for me. Much less would I send away, for the sake of a little money, a man grown old in my service, from his usual place and food. To him, poor man! it would be as bad as exile, since he could be of no more use to the buyer than he was to the seller. But Cato, as if he took a pride in these things, tells us that, when consul, he left his war-horse in Spain, to save the public the expense of carrying him.

You will agree with me, girls and boys, that the spirit of Plutarch was nobler than the spirit of Cato. You will be interested to hear that Plutarch was very proud of his little daughter's goodness of temper. "When she was very young," he says, "and had fed at the nurse's breast, she would often ask the nurse to feed also the other children, and the babies and dolls whom she looked upon as her servants."

Alas! Plutarch's little daughter died while she was still young.

THE GENERAL WHO ATE
DRY BREAD

"THE war in Africa is ended. The Roman eagles have again won great victories."

"Ah," said another Roman to him who had first spoken, "but though the southern foe is beaten, there is a worse foe on the north—beyond the white Alps."

"Who are they?"

"Men like giants, with blue eyes. There are two nations of them: the Cimbri and the Teutons."

"Have we a general who is strong enough to meet them?"

"Yes, we can trust the rough-handed and rough-voiced Marius. He is not a gentleman-soldier who loves to dwell in a tent with soft cushions. He shares with his men. When they have dry bread, he eats the same."

Marius was a man of the people. He lived 155–86 B.C. As a lad he worked in the fields. In the army he acted as a brave fighter, and he rose to be a clever captain, then general. Instead of choosing his warriors from among the land-holders, he chose poor men— men who owned nothing—men who were unemployed. He drilled them; he taught them to bear hardships; they would go anywhere and do anything for Marius.

Near the Alps the Romans had fixed their camp. Two vultures had flown over their heads, and as the birds flapped their wings the Romans shouted for joy. They said it was always a sign of coming victory when the vultures saluted them. The birds had been caught some time ago, and small brass rings had been fastened round their necks so that they might be known again.

A river ran near the camp. The servants of the army needed water both for themselves and the oxen. They saw some of the Teutons on the banks of the stream. Nevertheless, they went with pitchers to the waterside, taking also their weapons. A skirmish took place on the bank of the river. The enemy quickly gathered their forces. First marched thirty thousand men, all belonging to one tribe, clashing their spears one against the other, and keeping up a roar of voices. Through the river splashed the blue-eyed Teutons. The Romans charged them. The struggle went on till the sun set, and the stars gleamed out over the hills and plains and the two camps.

By night Marius sent a band of three thousand men to steal behind the position of the Teutons, ready to fall upon them by surprise.

At dawn the Roman army began to descend the hill on which they had been encamped. Very slowly they stepped, their front firm as a wall. The fierce giants of the northern forests rushed again and again toward the Roman van, but were thrust back. A shout was heard in the woods behind the Teutons. The three thousand men in ambush issued forth in a rapid run. And now the Teutons broke at last. Thousands and thousands were the prisoners, and all the baggage fell into the hands of the victor Marius. This battle was fought in the year 102 B.C.

Next year (101 B.C.) Marius met the Cimbri in North Italy. Their horsemen were fifteen thousand, and they had helmets shaped like the heads of wild beasts, with nodding plumes; their breast-plates were of glittering iron, their shields of the same metal. From a distance they threw darts, and, when close, they fought with broad and heavy swords. These enemies, also, did the troops of Marius defeat. Strange was the sight which met the eyes of the Romans as they pursued the retreating Cimbri. The chariots at the rear of the host were filled with women and children. The women aimed arrows at the men that fled, thus slaying, perhaps, their own husbands, or sons, or fathers. They strangled their infants with their own hands; and, last of all, they killed themselves, sooner than fall into the power of the Romans. Such was the courage of the Cimbri women.

No wonder the people of Rome loved Marius, who saved them from the barbarians of the North. He was made consul five years running. And in all his government he showed that he cared rather for the people than for the lordly classes—the rich patricians, or aristocrats. A shrewd man named Sulla formed a strong party of patricians against Marius, and Marius was obliged to fly for his life to the coast and embark in a friendly ship.

You will smile at the way in which his grandson escaped from Sulla. The young man was in a house at night, packing up things which he thought would be useful to Marius in his exile. Time passed; the day dawned; a band of Sulla's horsemen appeared. One of the farmers of the estate saw them coming, and hurriedly hid the young fellow in a cart, which was loaded with beans. The farmer drove his oxen as fast as he could past the horsemen, who saw only the beans in the cart, and not the young Roman, who lay, with a fast-beating heart, underneath!

The ship that carried Marius touched at a point of the coast, and the general, who had been sea-sick, was glad to land. Meeting some countrymen who herded cattle, he asked for refreshment; but they, knowing Marius, said they had nothing to give him, and begged him to leave the district at once, lest Sulla in his wrath should destroy them for sheltering Marius. The ship sailed on. Next day, stopping again, Marius took refuge in a thick wood, sitting with his few companions among the trees, hungry and weary. But he never lost his spirit.

"Courage, my friends," he said. "When I was, but a child, an eagle's nest, with several young ones, fell into my lap. It was a sign that good-fortune would always come to me sooner or later."

A squadron of horsemen came in sight. Marius and his comrades ran to the beach and plunged into the sea, and it was as much as they could do to reach two ships which happened to be sailing close inshore. The pursuing horsemen shouted:

"You have Marius on board! In the name of Sulla we bid you yield him to us!"

The sailors first thought they would do so; then they thought otherwise. At length they said no. The cavalry departed, cursing as they went. But the sailors dreaded to keep the famous general in their charge. They said the wind was in the wrong quarter, and they must wait. Meanwhile Marius might rest at a grassy spot on shore. They landed him, and sailed away, leaving him all alone.

It was a dreary and desolate country. Marius scrambled over bogs and brooks, and saw a mean cottage in the midst of the fens. Throwing himself at the feet of the cottager, he asked for shelter, for he was trying to escape from foes.

"Come with me," said the good old peasant. Leading Marius to a cave by a riverside, he placed on the ground a bed of dry reeds, and bade the tired general rest there in safety. Soon, however, the noise of pursuers was heard. Marius hastened from the cave, and waded through the muddy marsh, up to his neck in the mire. He was soon discovered; and, soiled and damp, he was carried prisoner to the magistrates of the nearest town.

They resolved he should be put to death, and a man, sword in hand, entered the room where Marius was shut up, intending to slay him. The chamber was dark. Through the dim shadows could just be seen the figure of Marius, his eyes flashing with scorn as he cried:

"Dost thou dare to kill Marius?"

And such was the majesty of his look and voice that the would-be slayer was terrified, and fled, exclaiming:

"I cannot kill Marius!"

By this time a number of the townspeople had gathered in the hope of saving the general. They swarmed round the prison door.

"Let Marius go," they shouted; "it was he who preserved Italy!"

And he was set free, and the people led him to the sea-shore, and saw him on board a ship that was provided for him by one of his faithful followers. After a time he landed on the coast of Africa, at the place where broken walls and ruined towns showed that once the proud city of Carthage had stood. He hoped to receive help from the Roman governor of that region. But an officer from the governor came to say that Marius must at once leave the district, or else be treated as an enemy.

Marius sat thinking. He was sad at the idea that he should be driven from place to place like a wild beast. The officer asked what answer he should take.

"Tell your master," said the wanderer, "that you have seen the exile Marius sitting amid the ruins of Carthage."

I suppose he was reflecting how grand cities

may fall, as Carthage did, and how powerful statesmen may also fall from their high estate, as he himself had done.

And so the unhappy general set out on his wanderings once more. Sulla had departed to the East to wage war against the enemies of Rome in Asia. Marius deemed that now his chance was come. He landed on the coast of Tuscany, in northern Italy.

"I proclaim freedom to all slaves who will help me," he said to the people who met him on landing.

Not only slaves, but freemen also, came to his aid—peasants, shepherds, and other working-men. They thought Marius was the friend of the poor and humble. If he became master of Rome, the needy folk would enjoy good times. Marius soon had a great army. He marched toward Rome, posted his men on a hill overlooking the city, and prepared for the assault.

The senate (that is, the Council of Elders) sent a message to say the city should be surrendered.

And then followed a dreadful scene. A body of bloodthirsty men, specially chosen by Marius, went to and fro in the streets, killing all whom Marius marked out for death. If any man passed by and bowed to Marius, and the old general did not salute in return, it was taken as a signal of doom. The man was at once put to death.

Marius, however, could not forget his own deeds of horror. At night he lay tossing on his bed, thinking of the men he had slain, and thinking how Sulla would come back from Asia; and what then? And a voice seemed always to ring in his ears, saying over and over again the words: "Dread are the slumbers of the distant lion—Dread are the slumbers of the distant lion—Dread are the—"

And thus, feverish in his body and troubled in his mind, he lay sick, and died, aged seventy.

You see what disorder Rome was falling into when one party of the nation fought against the other.

It was a good thing for Rome that a strong will was soon to give order to the land, and give peace to the republic. This strong will was the will of Julius Cæsar.

THE RED GENERAL

"FIRE!" shouted the soldiers.

Fire, indeed, not of a burning house, but in the form of huge flames that shot up from a hole in the ground.

The whole army halted to watch the strange sight, and the general, whose name was Sulla, called up the soothsayers to explain the meaning of the fire. They whispered among each other for a while, and then one of them spoke:

"General, just as this flame has shot up suddenly from the earth, so there will arise in Italy a noble man, brave and handsome, who will put an end to the disorders that trouble the Roman Republic."

Sulla smiled.

"That man is myself. As to beauty, my golden locks of hair are proof of that. As to courage, I have been through battles enough to show my mettle."

Perhaps the flames were a kind of volcanic fire.

Other strange omens (or signs) took place, and were supposed to foretell the terrible events that were to happen in Italy. One day, the sky being bright and clear, there came from the heavens the sound of a trumpet, loud and shrill; and yet no trumpet was seen! And on another day, while the Roman senate were sitting, a sparrow flew into the hall where they were assembled, with a grasshopper in its mouth. It bit the grasshopper in two. The diviners (or soothsayers) then declared this to be a sign that the people of Italy would be divided into two parties. The people were, alas! divided into two parties in war; but you need not believe in the tale of the trumpet. As to the other story, it was not a very wonderful thing that a sparrow should bite an insect into two parts!

The name "Sulla," or Sylla, means "red," and this Roman general was so named because his skin was of a strong red color. His eyes were blue and fierce. His temper was wilful and cruel. And yet he sometimes seemed to care only for mirth and jollity, and he would spend hours and days in the company of clowns and dancers. He lived from about 138 B.C. to 78 B.C.

The King of Pontus (in Asia Minor) was Mithridates (*Mith-ri-da-teez*), and he had sent his armies into Greece. The Romans sent Sulla to turn them out.

The Red General halted before a Greek city—it opened its gates; before another—it opened its gates; before another—it opened its gates. Everywhere the citizens had the sense to yield to Rome, for they knew Rome would be sure to master the King of Pontus. But the city of Athens would not yield. Sulla laid siege to the city. So resolved was he to take it that he brought up against its walls an immense number of siege-engines; so many that ten thousand mules were employed to draw them. Being very eager to obtain money to carry on the war, he sent a messenger to the famous temple of Apollo the Sun-god at Delphi (*Del fi*), bidding the priests give up their treasures.

"Hark!" said the priests to the messenger, "do you not hear the sound of a lyre? It is the Sun-god himself who strikes the strings and makes music in the inner chamber of the temple."

The messenger wrote a letter relating this story to Sulla. The Red General laughed, and replied that the Sun-god was playing a melody to show how pleased he would be to oblige Sulla with his gold! So the poor priests had to surrender their precious store, and even had to hand over a huge silver urn which they prized very much.

Meanwhile the people of Athens were starving. They had to eat roots, and even gnawed leather. The commander of the garrison at last sent out some men to beg for peace. But they stupidly talked in a boastful manner about the great heroes who fought for Athens in the olden days.

"Go, my noble souls," said Sulla to them, in a sneering tone, "and take back your fine speeches with you. I was not sent to Athens to learn its ancient history, but to chastise its rebellious people."

Soon afterward the city was taken, and many were the slain in its streets.

An army of the King of Pontus held a strong position on a rocky hill. Two Greeks came to Sulla, and offered to lead a band of men to the top, so as to surprise the foe from the rear. Sulla gave them a small troop of Romans. They climbed a narrow path, unobserved by the Asiatics. Sulla attacked in front. The Romans at the summit of the mountain raised a loud yell, and began to descend. The enemy hurried down, springing from rock to rock, only to be met by the spears of Sulla's legions. Fifteen thousand men in the Asiatic army were slaves. They had been promised their freedom if they beat the Romans; but only a few of them escaped with their lives.

Not long afterward a second battle was fought. The foe were posted near a marsh. Sulla ordered his men to cut trenches, so that these ditches should keep the Asiatics from escaping one way, while his horsemen drove them toward the muddy marshes in another direction. But the enemy set furiously upon the diggers, who fled in confusion. Then the Red General seized a wooden eagle from a standard-bearer, and pushed his way through the runners, crying:

"Yonder, Romans, is the bed of honor I am to die in! When you are asked where you deserted your general, mind you say it was here!"

These words roused a sense of shame in his men. They rallied to his support, and the struggle ended in another victory for the soldiers of the republic. Soon Greece was free from the power of Mithridates, and he was fain to make peace.

Sulla suffered from the gout, and he betook himself to a hot spring, the waters of which were said to have a healing effect; and there he bathed his swollen feet, and lived lazily for a while, and sported with his dancers and buffoons.

When on his march to the shores of the Adriatic Sea, on his return to Italy, he passed a place where the grass and trees were of a most beautiful green. And here was brought to the Red General a most peculiar-looking person—a Wild Man of the Woods—who had been found asleep on the ground.

"This is a satyr," said the people, who led the strange creature to Sulla.

A satyr (*sat-ir*) was often carved by the old Greek sculptors. They made him appear as a mischievous-looking man, with a pug nose, curly hair, ears with pointed tips like goats' ears, and short tail. The satyrs used to play travellers in the woods many tricks, and then laugh at the vexation they caused. According to the story, the satyr who was shown to Sulla could not talk any language. He was asked questions in Latin, in Greek, in Persian, but all to no purpose; he replied in a noise that sounded like the neigh of a horse or the bleat of a goat. Sulla was shocked at the sight, and ordered the so-called satyr to be taken away.

Well, it was indeed sad to see this deformed creature, and hear his harsh voice. But what shall we say to Sulla himself? He had the form of a man; his limbs were well-shapen; his mind was clever; yet his deeds were brutal. When he arrived in Italy he made his way toward Rome. It was his intention to crush down the people's party—the plebeians. He belonged to the upper class, or patricians. All over Italy there were brave and honest men who worked hard in field or trade, or served in the Roman armies, and yet were not allowed to rank as freemen, and had no vote in public affairs. Many of these men had raised a rebellion, and some had received the title of freemen; but there was still sore discontent over the land, and great was the hatred between the mass of the common folk and the rich patrician class to which Sulla belonged.

A battle took place close to the walls of Rome. Sulla won, and entered the city. There is a dreadful tale that he had six thousand prisoners crowded into a yard and all put to death, and that he made a speech to the Roman senate while the cries of the unhappy prisoners were plainly heard. He had lists of citizens written up in a public place, the lists being the names of "proscribed," or condemned, citizens. All must die, and their property was given to strangers. One day eighty were proscribed; the next day, two hundred and twenty; the third day, two hundred and twenty more. He declared himself dictator, having all power of life and death. The people's party were in deep distress; the patricians were glad.

When he thought he had quite cowed the people's party he gave up his high office, and lived as a common citizen, and walked about the streets without a guard. Then he retired to a villa at the seaside, and died in the year 79 B.C. At his funeral a vast amount of cinnamon and other sweet spices was burned. But his memory was not sweet. Who could love the memory of a man who had caused so much pain and grief?

Rather would we honor the memory of a Roman in a certain city which was doomed by Sulla. An enormous number of captives, whom Sulla called rebels, were ordered to be slain—all except one, at whose house the Red General had once passed some agreeable hours.

"No," said this noble Roman, "I will not live while so many of my fellow-citizens die unjustly."

And he mixed with the people, and his dead body lay with theirs. His name is unknown, but we will salute the nameless hero.

BATTLE-FIELDS AND GARDENS

THE snow fell fast and thick. Ten cohorts of Roman foot-soldiers (a cohort was about six hundred men) were struggling through the storm. There were also cavalry soldiers, and their horses slipped on the frosted ground. Some men sank in the drifts, overcome by the cold. But the general, Lucullus (*Lu-kul-lus*), who lived from about 110 B.C. to about 57 B.C., bade the army go on in spite of the tempest. They caught up the enemy—the army of Mithridates, King of Pontus, and killed many, and took fifteen thousand prisoners.

The King of Pontus escaped by water, and sailed with many galleys on the Black Sea. A storm arose. Many of his ships were wrecked, and broken timber and rigging strewed the shores for miles. The royal galley was filling with water. A boat rowed by Black Sea pirates was passing, and the king was glad enough of their help to reach the coast of Pontus.

The Roman general was a man of strong will. You see how he could make a king fly for his life, and his own soldiers would dare snow, hail, wounds, and death at his command.

When the King of Pontus renewed the war he pitched his camp on a plain among the mountains and forests. The Roman camp was not far off. One day some of the king's men ran, with loud shouts, after a deer. A number of Romans rushed from their camp to attack the Asiatics. A skirmish took place. The Romans began to retreat.

Lucullus had watched the fight from the wall of his camp (for you know the camps were surrounded by walls of earth, with gates in them). Alone he leaped from the wall, and walked toward the place of battle.

"Halt!" he cried to the first men that came up.

They halted; the rest rallied also. They made a firm stand against the enemy, and in the end drove them back to their camp.

But Lucullus was not satisfied. He called together all the army. The men who had fled from the foe were ordered to strip off their coats and girdles, and dig a trench twelve feet long. The rest of the soldiers watched the digging. This digging was counted a great disgrace.

A few days afterward the Romans burst into the Asiatic camp. The king's troops gave way in panic, snatching plunder even from their own friends. One of their own captains was slain for the sake of the purple robe he wore. King Mithridates was swept along in a crowd of soldiers that were pushing through a gateway of the camp. The Romans were close upon him when a mule happened to trot by. On its back was a sack of gold. The pursuers at once seized it, and quarrelled with one another as to who should have the yellow metal. Meanwhile the king escaped.

Step by step, the Romans became masters of all Asia Minor. The King of Pontus fled to his son-in-law, Tigranes (*Tig-ra-neez*), king of the hilly land of Armenia. A Roman named Appius was sent to the court of the King of Armenia.

This king kept great state. Whenever he rode out four footmen in short jackets ran before him, fleet as horses. These footmen had once been kings themselves.

Tigranes sat on his throne. The four kings stood by with their hands clasped together as a sign of their slavery. A large number of courtiers wore splendid robes.

Appius the Roman glanced round the shining throng without fear.

"I come, sir," he said, "from my chief, Lucullus. He asks you to give up to him the person of Mithridates, King of Pontus."

"What for?" asked the king, trying to look as if he cared naught for the Roman power.

"To follow in the train of Lucullus when he goes through the streets of Rome in triumph."

"And suppose I will not yield him up?"

"Then, sir, the Romans will declare war against you."

All the hearers wondered. Such bold speaking to

85

the king they had never heard before.

War was declared. Near the Taurus mountains, capped with snow, lay the chief city of Armenia. Tigranes had collected an immense host of horsemen, archers, and slingers. Thirty-five thousand pioneers were employed to level the roads, to build bridges, and to provide wood and water for the warriors.

On the flat land by the river and the city was drawn the small army of Lucullus. Six thousand kept an eye on the city, eleven thousand prepared to attack the vast host of Tigranes.

From the hills the king looked down at the little band of Romans as it moved toward the river. His Armenians laughed at the smallness of the enemy's force.

"The Romans are afraid! They are marching away!" rose the cry.

It seemed so. Only one courtier thought otherwise.

"Sir," he said to the king, "the Romans do not put on their helmets and polish their shields so brightly when they wish to retreat."

Presently the Romans wheeled to the right. They had reached a ford. The foremost man, carrying an eagle, splashed into the river; and the rest followed in order.

"Are these men coming against us?" exclaimed Tigranes; and he hastily arranged his troops to meet the onset.

As Lucullus was about to enter the river, one of his officers said:

"Sir, this is a black day in Roman story. It was on this day—the sixth of October—that the Cimbri from the north once defeated our countrymen in Italy."

"I will make this day a happier one for the Romans," replied Lucullus.

The armies met in the shock of war. Lucullus, with a division of troops, climbed a hill, and called to his men:

"The victory is ours, my fellow-soldiers! The victory is ours!"

It was indeed. An awful mass of dead was left in the valleys; and yet (so it is said) the Romans only had five killed and one hundred wounded. Such was the defeat of the vain king who despised the fewness of the enemy.

Far among the Armenian mountains Lucullus pushed his way. Never had Romans been so far from home. They were toiling up rocky passes, slipping over snow-drifts, tramping through great and lonely forests. At length their patience gave out. There could be no use in conquering more of this wild region. Lucullus heard their murmurs, and ordered a retreat.

Not long afterward he returned to Rome, and his place in Asia Minor was taken by the famous general Pompey.

Grand was the triumph of Lucullus in the city

of Rome. In the procession were to be seen ten Asiatic chariots, armed with scythes attached to the wheels; sixty captive nobles; one hundred and ten galleys with brass beaks in front (these, of course, were drawn on wagons); a statue of King Mithridates, all of gold, six feet high; twenty loads of silver vessels; thirty-two loads of gold cups and coins; eight mules carrying gold bedsteads; fifty-six mules carrying lumps of silver, and one hundred and seven mules carrying silver money.

And now, after all these hard campaigns and victories, what do you think Lucullus did?

You have heard of the Bay of Naples—its blue sea, the hills draped with green trees and vines, and the mountain Vesuvius that rises behind. On this lovely coast the old Roman general had resolved to settle down—to eat, drink, and be merry. Here he raised a splendid villa, or mansion, with many chambers. All about the place you could see marble, gold, silver, rich purple carpets. Many slaves moved from room to room. Fountains shot up sprays of water to make the sitting-rooms cool and musical. At dinner the gentlemen ate while slaves played on sweet flutes. He had another villa near Rome, in which there was more than one great dinner-room, the largest being called Apollo.

One day, being in the forum at Rome, he met his two friends—Cicero, the orator, who lived from 106 B.C. to 43 B.C., and Pompey, the soldier.

"Good-day, Lucullus," said Cicero. "We have not spent an evening with you lately."

"Nothing would please me better than to entertain you to-night to dinner."

"Many thanks; but you are not to prepare a grand reception for us. We want to dine with you just in the ordinary way."

"My dear Cicero, you shall hear my orders to the servant. They will be very plain and simple." Calling a slave, he said:

"My two friends and I will dine in the Apollo this evening."

"Yes, sir."

That was all. But when they reached the villa the Apollo chamber was decked with gold, silver, purple carpets. The dishes on the table were golden. Bands of musicians played. Dancers danced on the polished floor. Roses were scattered. The feast cost many thousands of dollars.

Lucullus had rooms fitted up for books, and scholars (or learned men) might come in and read, or sit under the portico and discuss. He had galleries full of pictures and statues, which cost vast sums of money.

Round his villas he had great gardens laid out, where you could sit under the shade of cedars; where the palm rose high over myrtles and fig-trees; where flowers formed lovely beds; where fountains glittered; where people could walk along winding paths, under archways of green. And in his gardens at Naples, Lucullus built big ponds, the water coming from the neighboring sea, and in the ponds large numbers of fish were kept.

Such were the villas and gardens of Lucullus.

Was it right of him to spend so much wealth on such pleasures?

Perhaps you say the money was his own. He had won it in the wars.

He had certainly fought hard in the wars; but so had his army, and they went home from the battle-fields to hard toil in the fields, and to mean houses. And, besides this, masses of people in Italy were poor and needy. Was it right to feast so grandly while these people were in such different circumstances?

Again, the villas and gardens could not be kept up without slave labor. Behind the splendor of the house there were hid a host of men and women who were not free.

And again, the villas and gardens were the private property of one man. If they had been made beautiful for the whole of the people to enjoy, we might admire them more. Even then I cannot see that life is any more bright and joyous for so much gold and silver.

Do not forget, also, that the wealth of Lucullus was robbed from the folk of Asia. How many of them had to live more wretched lives and pay more taxes because of the gardens of Lucullus!

THE MAN WHO LOVED GOLD

HIGH and rugged cliffs rose above the sea-beach. Amid the rocks could be seen a dark opening, which was the entrance to a cave. The waves rippled up the sand, and splashed about the rocks near the cave's mouth.

A man, carrying a large basket, came along the beach. He looked round to see if he was watched. At the entrance to the cave he laid the basket down. Then he quickly departed. The sun was setting.

A Roman, dressed as a servant, presently appeared at the cave's mouth, picked up the basket, and went in again. If we could have followed him, we should have seen him pass into a large chamber which the sea had formerly worn in the body of the rock; then into a smaller chamber beyond. Here sat his young master, Crassus, who lived from about 105 B.C. to 53 B.C., with about a dozen other Romans. The basket was opened. Provisions were taken out, and the party ate their supper heartily, leaving some of the food for the morrow.

Each evening for eight months the same thing happened. The party in the cave were hiding from the wrath of Cinna, who was putting to death those who opposed his plans. Crassus and his companions had fled from Rome to Spain, and found refuge in the cave. The owner of the land near the cave was his friend, and sent a steward every day with the food. There was plenty of room in the cave, there being several other recesses, or chambers, besides those I have mentioned.

At length, when Cinna was dead, it was safe to come forth from the hiding-place. Crassus belonged to a well-known family in Rome, and he rose to be a leader of the people. There were at this time three notable men in Rome—Pompey, 106–48 B.C.; Julius Cæsar, 100–44 B.C., and Crassus.

Of all things in the world Crassus was most fond of riches. He had an immense number of slaves, and many of them were clever men, able to read, write, and teach; and he sold these teacher-slaves for a much higher price than he gave for them, for such teachers were wanted to give lessons to boys in rich families. He owned very many houses in the narrow streets of Rome, and the rent brought him a large income. Every year he gained more wealth.

Crassus led an army against the slaves who rebelled. Some of the rebels were gladiators—that is, prisoners taken in war, and trained to fight in the circus before a vast crowd of onlookers. In these circus fights the gladiators were often slain. The leader was Spartacus (*Spar-ta-kus*). He also had herdsmen and shepherds among his followers. In more than one battle the slaves had won, and Spartacus had bright hopes of gaining freedom for his army. Before his last battle, in 71 B.C., he drew his sword and killed his horse, saying:

"If I am victor in this fight, I shall have plenty of horses; if I am defeated, I shall have no need of this."

Through a shower of arrows the captain of the gladiators rushed to find Crassus, the Roman general. Two officers sought to stay his valiant course, but he killed them both. Then he was surrounded by foes, and died. Spartacus was a martyr. He died while trying to obtain liberty for the slaves. So I do not think there was glory for Crassus in this victory.

And still his love for gold increased.

Once, indeed, when he and Pompey were elected consuls of the Roman Republic, Crassus gave a feast to the people of the city. The guests sat at ten thousand tables. You might think from this that he was generous. But his heart was set on getting a great honor, and that honor would lead on to more gain of gold. And he feasted the people in order to win their support.

Cæsar was made governor of the broad land of Gaul for five years. Pompey was put in command of the mountains and fertile fields of Spain. Crassus was chosen chief of the army which was to fight the fierce Parthians on the farther side of the river Euphrates (*U-fray-teez*), more than a thousand miles from Rome. His heart was glad. This was the honor he had dreamed of. He thought of himself as crowned with victory, and master of the gold and treasure of the East.

"To the East! To the East!" so his heart kept repeating.

A grand army marched with him across Asia Minor. They built a bridge across the stream of the Euphrates. Many castles and towns yielded. One small city closed its gates. The Romans soon captured it. Crassus was overjoyed at winning this little fortress. The soldiers shouted to him:

"Imperator! Imperator!"

This is to say, "Great Commander." And the foolish man was flattered and pleased. He sent his officers into all the cities to make notes of the amount of money in the public treasury or the gold in the temples. Already he was reckoning up his profits.

Crassus was now making his way along the high ground near the river. Boats followed to supply his troops with food and other needs.

One day an Arab chief visited the Roman camp, his eyes black, his hair black, his skin bronzed by the sun, a loose cloak hanging over his head, shoulders, and back.

"Sir," he said to Crassus, "I never saw a more splendid army than yours. Why do you wait? The enemy are losing heart. I have seen them in their camp on yonder plain. Your Roman soldiers are now full of spirit. I advise you to descend from the hills and strike the great blow at once. You are sure to win."

Ah, he was a traitor. He had been sent by the Parthians.

When the Arab offered to lead the Romans by an easy path to the plain, Crassus eagerly agreed.

At first the road was easy and smooth for the foot-soldiers and horsemen and camp-followers. After a while they found themselves on a wide desert, and they tramped, weary and thirsty, over hillocks of sand. No brooks gave water; no trees gave shelter. The Arab presently left the Romans to look after themselves.

The Parthian commander was a fine, tall man, with curly hair. He led his army in proud calmness. He was sure of winning.

The Romans were arranged in an immense square. Slowly they moved forward. Many of them murmured: "We ought to have stayed on the hills."

The Parthians advanced, beating their drums. These were made with leather, and were hung with small bells, so that the drums thumped and the bells rattled at the same time. All of a sudden the Parthian warriors threw off their coats and capes, and their armor flashed with a terrible light. They came toward the Romans. Presently they appeared terrified, and ran back. The Romans followed. The Parthians turned, and shot poisoned arrows while they fled. That was the custom of the Parthians—to shoot while flying. Their supply of arrows was enormous. They had camels loaded with these weapons, so that they could keep up a rapid discharge.

Young Crassus, son of the general, pursued a body of the flying foe. They halted and faced him, and threw up a cloud of dust and sand, so as to make it difficult to see them. The young leader was slain, and before long the enemy held up his head in sight of the elder Crassus. The old general walked up and down the ranks, begging the Romans to keep up their courage. All through the day the soldiers of the republic did indeed do their best. They had courage, but they had lost faith in their general.

Night fell. Mournful was the silence in the Roman camp. Crassus had covered his head with a cloak, and lay on the ground without speaking. Some of his captains called a council of war, and determined to break up the camp. Without the signal of trumpets the Romans stole away in the darkness, leaving many of the wounded to their fate.

The sentries at the gates of a city heard in the night a man's voice calling to them in Latin to open. It was the first of the retreating army. The city was held by a Roman garrison. Here for a few days the defeated soldiers rested.

Then they set out again toward the hill-country. A guide led them among bogs, where the Romans and their horses floundered in mud. With much hard labor they struggled through to the rising ground. Soon afterward the Parthians' host came up, and the general invited Crassus to come and talk over terms of peace. Crassus was not willing.

"You must go!" cried his men. "You sent us to fight the Parthians. Are you not ready to meet them when they come to make peace with you?"

He descended the hill, with a few of his attendants. They all went on foot.

"What!" cried the tall leader of the Parthians, "do I see a Roman general on foot? You must have a horse."

A horse with golden harness was led forward, and Crassus mounted, and rode a little way with the Parthians. The army watched from the hillside, and they saw a scuffle begin. Blows were exchanged. The Romans fell. A Parthian presently carried the head of Crassus in his hand.

I need not tell the rest of the sorrowful tale. It is said that in the battle on the plain and during the retreat twenty thousand Romans were killed and ten thousand taken prisoners.

Yes, we should pity the Romans. We should also pity the far larger numbers of people in Asia, Africa, and Europe whom the Romans slew in their conquests.

Crassus also deserves our pity. How he had set his heart on riches! How he had looked forward to being lord of Parthia, and adding its gold and treasure to his store!

In the history-books he is called Crassus the Rich.

But was he really rich?

Do you know what I mean?

THE WHITE FAWN

"HURRAH!" shouted the Spaniards who were watching from the walls of a city. "Our brave fellows are coming back! They are waving their swords! They have beaten Sertorius and his Romans!"

"Open the gates!" cried others.

The citizens streamed out, raising joyful cheers. But what was their terror when, all of a sudden, their supposed friends fell upon them, killing and wounding right and left!

The leader, Sertorius, was a most wily man. He had disguised his soldiers in Spanish dress, and thus deceived the citizens. Soon the town was in the hands of the Romans, and many of the inhabitants were sold into slavery.

I said he was wily. But not cowardly. He faced danger without flinching. In one of his battles he lost an eye. He used to speak proudly of his loss.

"Ah," he said, "some warriors have chains and crowns as a reward for their victories. But they cannot always wear the chains and crowns, while I carry my token of battle about with me!"

For a while Sertorius stayed in Rome, hoping to rise to a place of power. But Sulla, the Red General, was his foe, and he deemed it wise to retire to Spain, where he held out against Sulla's rule. The Red General sent armies to subdue him, but Sertorius, as clever as he was brave, succeeded in escaping by sea. A violent storm nearly broke up his fleet of ships. He landed again in the south of Spain, near the water-passage now known as the Strait of Gibraltar. At this point he met a party of seamen, who had just come back from the western sea.

"Where have you been?" he asked these sailors.

"Sir," they said, "we have been on the great sea, as far as the Fortunate Islands, a thousand miles from here."

"What kind of islands are they?"

"Rain seldom falls there; the breeze blows soft; the air is sweet; the soil is rich. We think these islands must be the Happy Fields of which the poet Homer sings."

"I will go and see this happy land for myself," said Sertorius.

But his plan was never carried out. He crossed to Morocco, and helped the prince of the Moors to regain his lost throne; and while he was in Africa a message came to him from Spain.

"We look to you," was the message, "as our captain, to defend us against the Romans."

So here was a Roman, acting as leader of the

Spanish people against his own republic. This was not because he hated his own country, but because he thought Rome had fallen into the power of men who would do no real good.

One day a Spaniard brought to General Sertorius a beautiful young deer. The little creature was white all over, and soon became attached to her Roman master, following him about like a dog, even amid the clash and bustle of the camp. At length the idea occurred to him that he might make great use of the white fawn. He told the Spaniards this creature had been given him by the huntress Diana, goddess of the crescent moon.

One day he brought out the white fawn covered with flowers.

"Victory! victory!" he cried to the Spanish folk who crowded round. "My troops have gained a victory over the army of Sulla."

"How do you know that, sir?"

"My friend the fawn has told me so."

"Can the creature speak?"

"Yes. The goddess Diana has given it the power to tell me secrets."

The simple Spaniards believed the story. As a matter of fact, news of the battle had been brought to him by a messenger; and he kept the tidings quiet till after he had led out the white fawn. Then the messenger appeared in public, as if he had only just arrived, and gave out the news of the victory! No doubt Sertorius found the fawn useful in making him seem very wise; but he was deceiving the poor Spaniards.

Four Roman generals were in the field against him; but so cunning and quick was Sertorius that he defeated each, though they had one hundred and twenty thousand footmen, six thousand horsemen, and two thousand bowmen and slingers. When the Spaniards were hard pressed by the enemy they took to the mountains, where the heavily armed Romans could not follow. Sertorius, like his Spanish soldiers, could bear much hardship. He could sleep on the bare ground, or even, if need be, could go without sleep several days and nights running; his food was very plain, and he drank no wine. He drilled the Spaniards after the Roman manner, and allowed them to use golden ornaments for their helmets and shields. In one city he set up a fine school, where the sons of Spanish chiefs were taught by Roman teachers to speak and read and write Latin and Greek. The pupils of the school wore coats with purple edging.

Some of his Spanish and Moorish troops did not fall in with his ideas about order and discipline. They wanted to rush into battle in their wild, native way, each fighting for himself, and thinking that the force of blows was sure to win, never troubling about moving at the general's command. One day these disorderly warriors were badly beaten by the steady-eyed and steady-handed Romans; and at the end of the day they sat round their camp-fires, unhappy and hopeless. A few days afterward Sertorius taught them a lesson. Before his assembled army he had two horses led out, one weak and old, the other strong and big, with a large tail. A small man stood by the big horse, and a tall, burly man stood by the weak horse.

"You two men," said Sertorius, "are each to pull out the tail of the horse you stand by."

The big man tugged at the little horse's tail with all his might, but could do nothing, and the crowd of warriors shrieked with laughter.

Meanwhile the small man was quietly picking out the tail of the big horse, one hair at a time, till the tail was all gone! Then Sertorius spoke:

"My friends, you who dash madly into battle, without heed and without sense, are like the big fellow who tugs and tugs and gains nothing. The other man has used less force of muscle, but he has used more intelligence; he has thought out a wise plan, and stuck to it till it succeeded."

The Spaniards understood, and paid more attention to his directions. They saw that wit was often more valuable than brute strength.

For instance, he led his troops against the hill-tribes who lived by robbing villages and cities. The robbers lived in caves, as some Spanish gypsies do to this day. The soldiers of Sertorius could not climb up the steep paths and capture the robbers, who retired like rabbits to their burrows. The general noticed that the clay in that district was light and crumbling and dusty. He also observed that, at certain times, the north wind blew. So he bade his men heap up clay, and stamp on it, and let the horses trample up and down it, until great clouds of dust arose, which was blown by the north wind into the robbers' caves. The hill-folk could scarcely breathe for the dust, and had to surrender.

Once the white hind was lost (for the fawn was now grown into a hind), and Sertorius was in much trouble. Some of his soldiers found her, and brought her to the general. He told these men to say nothing about it, and for a few days he kept the animal in hiding.

He called the Spaniards together for a public meeting about the business of the country. He seemed all smiles.

"I feel sure," he said to the Spanish chiefs, "that a great good-fortune will happen to me to-day. I have been told so in a dream."

Just then a servant let the hind loose. It ran out to its master, and licked his right hand. The Spaniards shouted themselves hoarse in their surprise and pleasure!

These tricks do not show Sertorius in the best light. He did what many clever people have done: he made a profit out of the ignorance of people less intelligent than himself.

But another story will show the nobler side of his nature. Sertorius had made himself so powerful, and he was so respected by the native chiefs, that they resolved to elect him Prince of the Spanish nation. They were about to offer him this honor in an assembly of the tribes. Just then news came to him that his mother had died. His father had died many years before, and the mother had brought him up with much loving care. Sertorius retired to his tent. For seven days he would not come forth. Each day his officers came to the door and begged him to come among the people. But he lay on the ground in sign of deep mourning, and would not appear in the assembly until the week was ended.

He had now a kind of council to assist him in the government, which he called a senate; and such was his fame that the King of Pontus, the great Mithridates, sent and offered him his friendship.

At length, however, his Roman officers and senators became jealous of his high rank and power. As he sat at supper one evening in 72 B.C., he was slain by the hands of assassins.

What happened to the white hind I do not know.

THE CONQUEROR OF PIRATES

"I AM a Roman!"

"A Roman, sir? We beg your pardon, sir. O, kind Roman, forgive us for making you prisoner!"

With this cry the pirates fell on their knees, and smote their thighs with the palms of their hands. Some ran to tie his shoe-buckle; others brought him the toga, or gown, that had been dragged off his shoulders.

It was only done in mockery. These wild sea-robbers were at war with Rome and all the world. They had no fear of Romans.

Presently the prisoner was led to a ladder at the side of the big galley.

"Go in peace," said the pirates, with a sneer.

The Roman shrank from stepping down into the water. He was pushed forward, and fell into the sea and was drowned.

These pirates came from Cilicia, a province of Asia Minor, where they had whole villages and towns in their possession, as well as castles on the hilltops. Large numbers of persons who were discontented with Roman rule joined the roving warriors of the sea, and their galleys swarmed all over the Mediterranean. They made sudden attacks on cities on the coast, and at one place seized and carried off two officers (prætors) and their servants. And they plundered the holy temples of Apollo and other gods. Their ships were shaded by purple awnings, the back parts were gilded, the oars were plated with silver, and bands of musicians played while the pirates drank and danced. So much damage was done by this navy of robbers, who swept the sea from Syria to the Pillars of Hercules (Strait of Gibraltar), that the senate of Rome discussed means of putting an end to the pirate power. They resolved to send Pompey to do this dangerous work. Great was the joy of the citizens when they heard that Pompey was to take command. They had faith in his skill and courage.

In three months he had cleared the sea of these troublesome folk. He had five hundred galleys. He divided the whole Mediterranean Sea into thirteen parts, and placed a lieutenant over each, with a portion of the fleet. Then, sailing and rowing from the west, Pompey advanced, driving the pirates before him—eastward, eastward—fighting and capturing as he went, till the last of the robber ships surrendered. Pompey landed troops in Cilicia, and engaged in battle with the last of the pirate tribes. After his victory the villages, towns, and forts yielded. He had taken ninety ships with beaks of brass. There were twenty thousand prisoners, but instead of slaying them Pompey showed a merciful spirit, and placed them as colonists in various cities in Asia Minor and Greece. This was in 67 B.C.

Great were the wars of Pompey in Asia. He and his valiant Romans carried the eagles of the republic over rocky hills, over rivers, marshes, deserts, through forests, among wild tribes, among the Armenians, the Syrians, the Jews, the Arabs. They took a thousand castles and nine hundred cities.

Perhaps he would think to himself sometimes: "Some day I may be master of all the Roman world, from Spain in the west to the palm-trees of Arabia in the east."

Two other men, Crassus the Rich and Julius Cæsar, were also men of power. There was a senate of noblemen who still sat and talked in the forum at Rome, but they could not manage to govern so large a domain of land and sea, and many of them only thought how to make themselves and their families wealthy. The three generals, Cæsar, Crassus, and Pompey, divided the lordship among them—Cæsar commanded the army in Gaul; Pompey had Spain and Africa; Crassus went to the east, where he was slain, as I have already told you.

Pompey gave the people of Rome a grand theatre, and provided splendid shows. Five hundred lions were let out of cages, and fought in the arena, or open space, amid the shouts of the citizens; and eighteen elephants waged battle with armed men. The people cheered Pompey when he passed through the streets. One year he acted as consul. The rich people—the patricians—were on his side. He lifted his head in pride, and dreamed that he would be the highest man in Rome. Some of his friends said to him:

"Beware of Cæsar! He will return from Gaul, and try to make himself master of Rome."

Pompey smiled.

"If," he replied, "I only stamp my foot in Italy an army will appear."

Cæsar felt that Rome needed one strong will to put the State in order, and to give just rule to the far-off provinces—Spain, Africa, Asia, Greece, and the rest. He was ready to take up the task. By rapid marches he brought his army to Rome. Thousands of Pompey's soldiers left him, and went over to Cæsar's side.

The senators ran to Pompey. One of them cried out:

"O Pompey, you have deceived us!"

Another bade him stamp on the ground to make an army appear, as he had once boasted he was able to do.

Before long Pompey had fled from Italy, his troops crossing the sea in five hundred ships to the hill-country north of Greece. He had seven thousand horsemen, all men of rich and noble families, and masses of foot-soldiers.

Among others who joined Pompey was Tidius Sextius, a lame old man, who came limping into the camp. Many of the soldiers laughed at this crippled warrior. They thought he could be of little use in the war.

But Pompey had a generous spirit. He rose up and ran to meet him, and showed Sextius much courtesy. He considered that a man who would give up the

POMPEY & TIDIUS·SEXTIUS

comfort of his home, and come to the wars for the sake of a friend, deserved honor and respect. Early one August morning, in the year 48 B.C., the red cloak—the signal of battle—was hoisted over Cæsar's tent on the plain of Pharsalia (*Far-say'-lia*). Pompey's tents were adorned with myrtle leaves; the soldiers' beds were strewn with flowers; wine-cups were set ready on the tables for a feast. The patrician knights made sure of victory over Cæsar's common bowmen and swordsmen. The haughty spirit of Pompey's men was soon to be broken.

Cæsar said to his foot-soldiers:

"Keep your javelins in your hands till Pompey's horsemen are close upon you. Then aim your short spears at their faces. These young gentlemen will not care to let the steel touch their fair cheeks."

And that happened. Pompey's cavalry recoiled from the shower of javelins, and they fled in panic. Before the day was out the army of Cæsar was rushing, like a mighty tide, upon the scattered troops of the man who had been called Pompey the Great.

Hurrying from the dreadful place of defeat, Pompey rode to a far valley, where he was glad to kneel by a brook and quench his thirst. Then he rode on—Cæsar and death were in pursuit. The blue sea came in view. On the shore, in a poor fisherman's cabin, the beaten general slept at night. At gray dawn he set off in a small river-boat, and was rowed along the coast till a friendly galley took him on board.

Cornelia, his wife, heard of his ruin. She lay a long time on the ground, without saying one word. His ship—he had but this one—lay in the harbor. At length she rose and went down to the sea. Pompey hastened to meet her on the beach. She hung upon his neck, exclaiming:

"Alas, my dear husband, that I should see you reduced to one poor galley. There was a time when you commanded five hundred vessels."

"Cornelia," he answered, "we have fallen from great things to this wretched condition; but we may also rise again to great things."

A number of his ships now sailed to his aid, and some of his followers had rejoined him. They resolved to cross over to Egypt. After a safe voyage, Pompey's small fleet lay at anchor off the Egyptian coast. Messengers were sent ashore to ask the young King of Egypt to grant shelter to Pompey.

One of the king's advisers said:

"If you receive Pompey, you will have Cæsar for your enemy. If you send him away, he may one day have revenge. The best plan is to invite him on shore and kill him. Dead men do not bite."

A small fishing-boat approached Pompey's galley. It contained only four or five men. They asked the general to go with them, and he did so.

They rowed in silence. Cornelia and her friends watched from the deck of the galley. Pompey sat reading a paper which he had written. He presently noticed that one of the rowers was a man who had served with him in the wars.

"I think you were once a fellow-soldier?"

The man only nodded in reply.

The boat touched the shore. Pompey placed his hand on the shoulder of Philip, his slave, and was about to step out. A stab from behind caused him to fall. Other blows followed. Pompey wrapped his cloak over his head, and lay on the sand and died. He was just fifty-nine years old.

A shriek was heard from the galley. Cornelia had seen the murder. A wind was springing up; the fleet set sail. Only a few slaves kept guard over the general's body.

Philip began to make a heap of wood for a funeral pile on which to burn the body of his master. An old Roman soldier, who had fought under Pompey many years before, happened to pass.

"Let me," he said, "assist you to do the last honors to the greatest general Rome has produced."

The next day the people who sailed along that coast saw the flames and smoke of the pile. Philip, the faithful servant, was standing by.

The head was not burned. It was kept till Julius Cæsar arrived. A man brought it to him as soon as he landed, thinking he would be pleased.

But no such thing. He turned his face away in horror.

Another person gave him Pompey's seal, with which the dead general used to stamp his letters and other papers. On the seal was engraved a lion holding a sword in its paws.

As Cæsar took the seal the tears came into his eyes. And in those tears you see the noble spirit of a Roman.

CAESAR AND HIS FORTUNE

"WELL, WELL, sir, we have got you now!"

"No doubt," said the young Roman, whom the pirates had just brought a prisoner to their island; "but of course you will let me go if my friends pay a ransom?"

"Certainly."

"How much do you ask?"

"Twenty talents" ($20,000).

"Is that all?" laughed Julius Cæsar. "I will promise you fifty."

He sent various friends to the nearest city where he was known to procure the money.

In the mean time he made himself at home among these fierce Cilician pirates, of whom I have told you in the life of Pompey. For thirty-eight days he dwelt on the island, and he treated the sea-robbers as if he were their lord, not their captive.

"When I am free again," he said to them, "I shall return here and crucify you."

They smiled at his frank talk.

The money arrived. Julius departed, got together a fleet of vessels, sailed back to the pirates' hold, and, true to his dreadful word, put them all to death. Young as he was, you see he had a stern and iron will. And if you think he was cruel toward the pirates, you must bear in mind that men in those old days (as is too often the case now) thought it right to crush enemies without mercy.

In Rome young Cæsar was famous for his ready tongue. Persons who needed defence against any that accused them were glad to have Cæsar to speak on their behalf.

He found his way to the hearts of the people. They admired Pompey, but they began to love Cæsar more. And one day he was to rise over all others, and stand as master of the Roman world, by sea and land.

You remember Marius, the general who ate dry bread. He was dead; but Cæsar, who was nephew to the wife of Marius, did not wish him to be forgotten. Marius had taken the side of the people against the proud patricians. Cæsar felt sure the Roman world was now too wide for these patricians to govern. He must win the mass of the people to his side, and get the power into his own hands, because he believed he could give order and peace to Italy, and all the other lands of the republic.

One morning some people entered the temple on the Capitol hill.

"See!" cried one, "there are some new statues!"

"And all of burnished gold!" exclaimed another.

"Whose figures are they?"

"Oh, I know this face! It is the face of the brave Marius. And here is writing below the statue. It says that the figures represent Marius overcoming the Cimbri of the North."

Before long immense crowds had swarmed up the hill to view the golden statues. The patricians frowned; the plebs (or common people) were joyful. It was soon known that Julius Cæsar had placed the figure of Marius in the Capitol.

Cæsar stepped from office to office—magistrate, chief priest, and then prætor, wearing the cloak with purple trimming. For a while he had a command in Spain. On his way to Spain he crossed the Alps. He and his troops marched by a little town.

"I wonder," said a friend, pointing to the group of houses on the hillside, "if the people there strive for the highest places, as men do in Rome?"

"Why not?" replied Cæsar. "I should do so if I dwelt in that town. I had rather be the first man here than the second man in Rome."

He carried on the war in Spain with much spirit, forcing the wild tribes to submit to the Roman eagles; and he led his legions as far as the Atlantic Ocean.

On his return to Rome he was elected consul. Then he took over the rule of Gaul—the country which is now the home of the great French nation, with the Belgians as their neighbors; but at that time it was parted among three hundred different tribes. And beyond the sea in the north was the land so often clothed in fog and beaten by contrary winds—the land of the Britons. In the plains and forests of this vast region the Romans—hard as oak, proud as kings, bold as lions—met the tribes, and grappled with them in many a dreadful struggle. It is said that Cæsar took eight hundred cities in Gaul, and engaged in various battles with three million men, a million of whom his armies slew, and a million were taken captive. Of course, we cannot be sure of the numbers, but the fact is clear that Cæsar conquered.

The general was slender in body. His health was not robust; sometimes his head ached painfully, and a fit would seize him. Yet nothing stayed him from his purpose. He set his face like a flint; and his men seemed to worship him, just as the French did with Napoleon long ages afterward.

For instance, in Britain the Romans met the natives in a marshy spot, and a band of Cæsar's men found themselves entrapped among the Britons. One of the Romans took the lead, hewed right and left among the islanders, beat them off, and rescued his comrades. Then he plunged into the stream that ran by, swam it, waded through the mud of the swamp, and reached the place where the general was watching. However, he lost his shield, and, in deep distress, he fell at Cæsar's feet, saying:

"General, I have lost my shield. I ask your pardon!"

As if he had done something disgraceful! Again, one of Cæsar's ships being captured off the coast of Africa, all the crew were put to death except one, to whom quarter (or mercy) was shown. But he was too proud to accept even life from an enemy. Exclaiming, "It is not the custom of Cæsar's soldiers to take quarter, but to give it!" he thrust a sword into his own breast.

Cæsar was not merely a strict commander. He took thought for the comfort of his followers so far as he could. One day he and some friends were on a journey. A storm burst, and, looking round for shelter, they spied a poor man's hut. To this they ran. There was only one room in the dwelling, and only space to take in one of the strangers. I suppose (though the story does not say) that the owner of the hut was himself present.

One of Cæsar's party, named Oppius, was taken ill. To Cæsar, as the person of highest rank, the bed in the hut was given; for the tempest howled, and it was plain that the travellers could fare no farther that night. But Cæsar yielded place to the sick man, and he himself, with the rest of his companions, slept under a shed that stood outside the cottage. Thus did Cæsar show his belief that it is the duty of the strong to help the weak.

When a battle was to be fought Julius Cæsar did not stand in an easy place while his soldiers bore the brunt of war. In his campaign in Gaul he was surprised by a sudden rush of the Helvetian tribes. Very hastily the Roman army drew itself into close array, and faced the foe. A page brought Cæsar's horse, but he would not mount.

"Take it away," he said to the attendant, "until the enemy retire, and until I need my horse for the pursuit."

So saying, the general charged on foot upon the natives; and his men, feeling that their leader was sharing the peril, did not flinch from the sharp conflict.

His hardest won battle was with the Nervii folk, in the thick forests of Belgium. The Romans were fixing their camp in the wood, digging trenches and stabling the horses, when sixty thousand Nervii, their shaggy hair streaming, raised a shout and attacked. Many Roman officers were slain. Cæsar snatched a buckler from one of his soldiers, and sprang forward to encourage his troops. At one moment it looked as if the whole Roman force would be crushed. The Tenth Legion were on a hill. Seeing the extreme danger, they hurried down, and turned the tide of battle.

Across the broad river Rhine, Cæsar built a large wooden bridge, in spite of the strong current of the water. Over this bridge the Romans marched, and thence made their way into the land of the Germans. The most savage region could not daunt them.

Beyond the sea lay the British Islands. The Romans had often talked about this far-off country.

"We don't believe there is any such place," said some.

"Oh yes," others would answer; "but it is so enormous a continent that it is hopeless to try and conquer it."

Julius Cæsar did not talk about it. He acted.

With a large fleet he crossed the water now called the English Channel. Soon Roman soldiers were seen carrying their eagles along the chalk cliffs of Kent, along the banks of old Father Thames, and in the forests beyond.

At length the time was come to return to Italy. The citizens of Rome were in very frequent tumult and fear. Pompey could not keep the love of the people. The noblemen of Rome—the patricians—had not the great hearts and great minds that were needed to sway so wide an empire.

"Oh, that Cæsar would come!" the folk whispered.

Cæsar led his splendid army through Gaul to the border of Italy, and halted at the little river Rubicon. Should he cross over to Italian soil? Should he declare war against his old friend Pompey, who had married Cæsar's daughter? Should he spill Roman blood? Dare he, like a player with dice, throw a die which might mean the loss of the grand game, and be his ruin?

He looked at the water; he looked at his friends. At last he plunged his horse into the stream, crying:

"The die is cast!"

Cæsar marched toward Rome—stern, calm, strong, like the rise of a tide which no man can stay.

In and out of the gates of Rome rushed people, on foot, on horseback, or carried in litters. "We are for Cæsar!" cried some.

"We are for Pompey!" cried others.

"We are for the patricians!" cried some.

"We are for the plebs!" cried others.

Thus the city was divided.

A Roman gentleman went to Pompey and said, with a sneer:

"Stamp with your foot, sir! You said once that, if you only did that, an army would spring up!"

Pompey did not stamp. He fled to the coast, and crossed the sea, and prepared the troops who gathered about him for the last stand against Cæsar. Now that he was master of Italy, Cæsar went over to Spain, and put down all men who sided with Pompey.

And now that he was master also of Spain he returned to Italy, was made consul by the Romans, and then set out to meet Pompey. So fast did he march to the eastern shore of Italy that the main part of his army lagged behind, and they murmured bitterly.

"It is winter," they said. "This man stops for neither wind nor hail. When will our labors be ended? Does he think our bodies are made of stone or iron? Our very shields and breastplates call out for rest!"

But when they reached the sea, and found that their general had already sailed for the opposite coast, they felt ashamed, and anxiously waited for the fleet to return and fetch them.

Cæsar, on his part, wished to bring his whole army together as soon as possible; for Pompey's legions were swarming on the land, and Pompey's ships sailing on the Adriatic Sea. One night he left his camp, entered a twelve-oared galley on a river, and bade the rowers hasten down to the sea as rapidly as they could. They worked hard. Cæsar, clad in a shabby cloak, sat silent and thoughtful. As the galley neared the mouth of the river the water became extremely rough, and hurrying clouds and darkened air made a terrible scene. The pilot trembled. He did not know Cæsar was on board, for the general wrapped himself close in the cloak.

"It is folly to go farther!" exclaimed the pilot. "We must turn back!"

Cæsar rose up, threw back his cloak, and said:

"Go forward, my friend, and fear nothing. You carry Cæsar and his fortune."

Like giants the oarsmen pulled against the storm. Cæsar's look and voice seemed to double their strength. However, nature is more mighty than man. The galley had to turn back and return to the camp. The troops were transported from Italy later on.

The armies of Pompey and Cæsar were now face to face. So spirited were Cæsar's men that, in spite of their want of food and other comforts, they showed a gay front. They dug up some eatable roots, soaked them in milk, and made a sort of bread—poor fare, but better than nothing. Some of them crept near Pompey's camp, and flung a number of these hard biscuits into the trenches, crying:

"So long as the earth yields roots we will resist Pompey!"

I have already told you of the battle of Pharsalia, 48 B.C., in which Pompey was beaten.

Cæsar's ships bore him to the land of the Nile and the Sphinx (Egypt), over which reigned the beautiful Queen Cleopatra, who lived from 69 to 30 B.C.

The tread of the Romans was next heard in Syria, and Cæsar's eagles were seen on the banks of the Jordan River.

News came that the Roman garrisons in Asia Minor were defeated by the Armenians. Cæsar at once pushed northward, across the Lebanon mountains, where the cedars grow, across the Taurus mountains, and as far as the plains of Pontus. One battle finished the war. When the victory was won, Cæsar sat in his tent and wrote a message to the senate of Rome. It contained (in Latin) but three words:

"Came—Saw—Conquered!"

He had come to Pontus; he had seen the enemy; he had beaten them. Cæsar's speech was terse—that is, he used only just enough words to make his meaning clear. Whenever you take a message, you should try to do likewise. See how few words you can say it in. Only, of course, you must not be too curt, else people will think you rude.

The next scene is in Africa, near the ruins of the city of Carthage. A large army of Numidians—barbaric horsemen who dwelt in the country now known as Algeria—threatened the Romans. So scarce was food for the horses at one time that seaweed had to be mixed with grass for the Roman steeds.

One day Cæsar's cavalry were resting. No enemy appeared in sight. The sound of a flute was heard. It was played by a black-skinned African, who danced to his own tune. The soldiers ran out of their camp, and sat round the African dancer, and laughed as he frisked about and rolled his eyes.

Suddenly a war-cry was heard. The Numidians had rushed out from a hiding-place. Many of the Roman cavalry were killed. The enemy even entered the camp. But Cæsar rushed forward, and the Africans recoiled and fled.

Not long afterward another engagement took place. An eagle-bearer was running away from the Numidians. Cæsar met him, seized him by the neck, turned him right-about-face, and said, quietly:

"Look on this side for the enemy!"

The final victory was won after a surprise. Cæsar led his men across rocky passes and through dark forests, and fell unawares upon the Numidian camp. King Juba fled in great haste, and Cæsar was lord of North Africa.

So now the time was come when he could go to Rome and enjoy a Triumph, while all the city shouted, "Yo! yo! yo!" In the grand procession through the streets walked the son of Juba, a young prince, who lived a long time in Rome, and became a writer of history and a great favorite of the citizens.

Cæsar entertained the people with feasts so large that the guests sat at twenty-two thousand tables. Combats of gladiators took place in the theatres.

Fights between ships also pleased the public, the ships being floated in immense ponds made for the purpose. The people now said to one another: "Pompey is dead, Crassus is dead; who is there able to govern the great Republic but Cæsar? Let us give all power into his hands."

He was made consul for the fourth time. Then he was made dictator, or master—lord of Rome, lord over the senate, lord of the armies, lord of all the Roman provinces. It would have been very easy for him now to take revenge upon his enemies. Their lands, their money, their houses, their lives—he could have taken all away, and none could withstand his will. But Cæsar loved Rome and the republic. He wished to heal her wounds. He wanted all the classes—aristocrats and the plebeians (or common folk)—to dwell in union. When the Roman senate saw how generously he behaved toward his foes, they ordered a new temple to be built to show their admiration of his spirit. The temple was built in honor of the goddess Mercy, or (in Latin) "Clementia."

Another high-minded act of Cæsar's was to raise up the fallen statues of Pompey. These figures had been flung down by his followers, but now they stood upright again for passers-bys to behold and to salute.

When Cicero, the famous speaker, saw this deed, he said:

"Cæsar has made himself a statue by raising up Pompey's."

Some of the patricians hated the new dictator.

They felt that he stood in their way, and prevented them from obtaining riches and command. Cæsar's friends knew of this hatred, and begged him never to go out without a body-guard.

"No," he replied; "it is better to die once than always to walk about in fear of death."

Cæsar would sit alone in his chamber and make great plans. He dreamed dreams of things he would do for Rome and for the world. He said to himself:

"I will march against the Parthians in the East, and against the Germans in the North, and bend them all to my will.

"I will dig through the neck of land by Corinth, so that ships may pass through a sea-canal.

"I will make the river Tiber deeper for big merchant vessels to bring their loads of corn and wine and oil to the gates of Rome.

"I will drain the filthy water out of the great marshes, so that pleasant fields may take the place of deadly swamps.

"I will build a dike along the western coast of Italy, and construct harbors in which hundreds of galleys may ride at anchor."

If he had lived, I believe he would have done all these things. But his life was cut short.

One thing, however, he was able to carry out, which should win our thanks to-day. The reckoning of days, months, and years had got into disorder. You hear people say that there are three hundred and sixty-five days in a year. So there are; but that is not the whole story. The people of Egypt long ago found out there were three hundred and sixty-five and a quarter days in a year. The Romans had not reckoned this extra quarter. Cæsar arranged that, as four-quarters of a day make a complete day, this extra day should be added to the year each fourth year. Thus we have what we call a leap-year of three hundred and sixty-six days. As Julius Cæsar set the calendar right, we name it the Julian calendar. And we may also note that one of the months—July—is so styled in his memory.

One day shouting and laughter were heard in the streets of Rome. It was the holiday known as the Lupercal (*Loo-per-kle*). Cæsar sat on a golden chair in the forum, and watched the lively crowds.

Presently his friend Antony came up to Cæsar, and, in view of the people, offered him a crown adorned with laurel leaves.

"O King, wear this crown!" said Antony.

Cæsar shook his head, and the Romans cheered loudly. They were pleased that he refused it.

Again Antony presented it. Again Cæsar declined. Again the Romans cheered. A third time Cæsar put the crown away from him. This incident reminds us how, many centuries later, the noble Cromwell refused the crown of England.

Some of Cæsar's foolish friends put crowns on the statues of Cæsar. Angry patricians tore them off. Cæsar's enemies whispered to one another that the time was come to check the tyranny. He must be slain.

Two of these whisperers were Brutus and Cassius. Often did they talk of the best way to get rid of the dictator. Their dark thoughts made them look pale and anxious. Cæsar noticed it, and (as we read in Shakespeare's play) he remarked to his friend Antony:

> Let me have men about me that are fat;
> Sleek-headed men, and such as sleep at nights.
> Yon Cassius has a lean and hungry look;
> He thinks too much; such men are dangerous.

Some of Cæsar's friends knew there was danger in the air, as people say. Indeed, tales were afterward told that men made of fire were seen fighting in the sky, and strange lights flashed across the heavens by night. You know how the Romans believed in such signs, or omens, which hinted at good or evil events about to happen. A certain man, said to be wise in omens, resolved to warn Cæsar. This soothsayer said to him one day:

"Beware the Ides of March!"

I must explain that each month of the year had in it a number of days called Ides; and in the month of March the Ides lasted from the eighth day till the end of the fifteenth—one week.

It was now the middle of March, in the year 44 B.C. Cæsar had supper with his friends, and then signed letters which his secretary brought to him. The guests were talking loudly.

"What are you conversing about?" asked Cæsar.

"The best kind of death. Which do you think the best?"

"A sudden one."

His death—a sudden one—came next day.

In the morning Cæsar—"the foremost man of all the world," as Shakespeare calls him—went out to the meeting of the senate. A crowd was in the streets.

"There goes Cæsar!" buzzed many voices.

He saw the soothsayer, and said to him: "The Ides of March are come!"

"Yes, but they are not gone!" replied the soothsayer.

A parchment, folded up, was thrust into Cæsar's hand.

"Sir, pray read it; it is most important," whispered a voice.

"Hail, Cæsar!" shouted the people.

"Make way for the dictator!" cried the officers.

Amid all this noise and movement he had no chance to read the paper in his hand; but on it was written a friendly message, warning him that certain patricians meant to take his life.

He entered the senate-house, and the elders rose to greet him. A statue of Pompey looked down upon the scene. Cæsar took his seat. Brutus, Cassius, and other senators gathered round. One bowed, and said:

"Sir, I beg of you to allow my exiled brother to

come back to Rome."

"It cannot be done. He is an enemy to Rome."

"Oh, sir, I beg of you!"

"No, I am resolved not to—"

A shout—a scuffle—a fall—Cæsar's cloak was dragged off his shoulders! Swords and daggers struck him. Cassius struck him. Brutus struck him.

And when his friend Brutus struck, Cæsar groaned, and lay down and died at the base of Pompey's statue.

Brutus and the other plotters marched, waving swords, to the Capitol, and crying:

"Freedom! freedom for Rome!"

"Freedom!" replied some of the passers-by; but many kept a gloomy silence.

Cæsar had wished to put an end to the power of a small group of men who boasted of their noble birth, and who wished to make themselves rich out of the broad empire which Rome had won. He wished Rome still to be the capital city; but he wanted to make the dwellers in Spain, Gaul, Greece, and other conquered lands, sharers in Rome's glory—to be citizens rather than beaten foes.

The day after the murder the body of Cæsar was carried through the streets of Rome, and through the forum.

The people heard Cæsar's will read to them. In this will he left much of his riches to the citizens. In death, as in life, he thought of others rather than his own enjoyment.

In Shakespeare's play the will is read to the people by Antony, who also shows them the wounds in Cæsar's body:

> I have neither wit, nor words, nor worth,
> Action, nor utterance, nor the power of speech,
> To stir men's blood; I only speak right on;
> I tell you that which you yourselves do know;
> Show you sweet Cæsar's wounds, poor, poor dumb mouths,
> And bid them speak for me!

The citizens then rushed away in fury to burn the houses of the plotters, and to slay them that had laid cruel hands on Cæsar.

A comet blazed in the sky for seven days after the murder. People gazed at it, and said it was a sign of the wrath of the gods at the evil deed of Brutus and Cassius.

A year or two later Brutus was preparing to fight his last battle against Antony and Augustus, and he lay in his tent, and the light of the lamp burned dim, as if in a fog. Then there stood beside the bed a strange, tall, and terrible figure, and it said:

"Brutus, I am your evil genius; you shall meet me at Philippi."

"I will meet you there," answered Brutus, boldly.

Then the ghost vanished into the night.

This story is, of course, only a legend. But you see it proves to us how the people of that time believed it was a wicked thing to slay Cæsar; and they thought it a just punishment upon Brutus that he should be beaten at Philippi. When Brutus saw the day was lost, he fell upon his own sword and died.

THE MAN WHO SELDOM LAUGHED

A ROMAN soldier held a boy in his arms at a window, threatening to drop him into the road below.

"Will you speak to your uncle for me?"

"No," replied the boy, "I will not."

"Not if I say I will let go unless you promise?"

"No."

The soldier set the boy down in safety inside the chamber, and said:

"This child is the glory of Italy."

He had been visiting the boy Cato's uncle, in order to ask his support. Many people in the Roman Empire who lived out of Rome wished to be made citizens, with a vote in the elections. The officer was acting as their spokesman. Half in fun, half in earnest, he had begged Cato to plead with his uncle on behalf of the would-be citizens.

You see what a fearless spirit the boy had.

When he was fourteen years old he happened to visit the house of Sulla, the Red General. He saw men carried out dead. They had been slain by the general's order, because they belonged to a different party in the State. Young Cato's anger was roused. He turned to his teacher, and cried:

"Why do you not give me a sword, that I may kill him, and rid my country of the tyrant?"

So fierce was Cato's voice that a friend of Sulla took alarm, and watched the lad closely lest he should attack the Red General.

Cato, 95 to 46 B.C., belonged to a patrician family—that is, he was of noble birth; and he had a fairly large estate. But he did not care to spend his money wastefully. He was a stern, strict man—one of the order called Stoics (*Sto´-icks*). Seldom did he laugh; seldom did he smile. Rich persons wore purple; and Cato, as if to show his scorn for their vanity, dressed in black. No matter whether the day was hot or cold, he would go without any head-covering; and he always walked barefoot. While his servants travelled on horseback, Cato trudged like a poor man. A friend in need was he, for he was no miser. He would lend money without expecting the payment of any interest. A friend also was he to the soldiers who fought under his command. Once when a war was ended and Cato was about to return home, the warriors who had served in his regiment spread their garments on the road for him to walk on, and kissed his hand as he passed, for he had won their love by his just treatment. Whenever he had set them a hard task, he had taken a part in the business himself.

Cato was elected a quæstor, or treasurer—that is, one of the keepers of the public money; and he was as careful of the city's money as if it was his own. If he found any man owed money to the city, he would bid him pay.

"But, sir," such persons would say, "this money was due as far back as twenty or thirty years ago. Surely you can take it as a thing forgotten now."

"No," replied Cato; "the money is owing to the treasury of Rome, and it must be paid."

On the other hand, if he found the city owed money to any man, he would see that the debt was paid, even though it had been left unthought of for many years. And so attentive was he to his work, that he was the first officer to arrive at the treasury in the morning and the last to leave at night. He did his business with all his heart and strength.

So true was he to his word that the Romans could readily trust whatever he said. At last a joke would pass among the people, and if one man told another a very wild story, the neighbor would shake his head and say:

"Well, gossip, I would not believe such a thing even if it were told me by Cato himself."

He did not believe in spending wealth too freely, even on men who gave delight in music or in acting in the theatres. Some rich folk would give a clever musician a crown of gold. But if Cato heard a beautiful piece of music played, he would call the performer to him, and offer him a crown of leaves from the tree known as the wild olive. If a man acted well on the stage, he would send him not jewels or vessels of gold and silver, but a parcel of beet-root, or lettuce, or radishes, or parsley, or cucumbers! I suppose he thought it was well to show his pleasure by a gift, but not to make such gifts as would render the musicians and actors greedy or vain. And perhaps he meant to hint to them that, after all, if a man did finely in his art, such as singing or reciting, he should be content with the honor in which he was held by the people, without wanting a present of money. For then it might be thought that he did his part skilfully, not because he loved his work, but because he loved the pay. Now, anybody could pluck leaves from a wayside tree and weave a crown of wild olive; but to win it as a prize in the public performance might make the artist justly proud, for he would be thinking more of the honor than of the reward.

Even for honors Cato did not greatly care. He had offered himself once to the Romans as consul, but he was defeated in the election. Many men who had failed to get the votes of the people would have gone home feeling very unhappy. But Cato went to the bath, rubbed himself in oil after the manner of the Romans, and had a hearty game at ball!

You have heard of the great war between Julius Cæsar and Pompey. In this struggle Cato took the side of Pompey and the patricians. When it was plain that Cæsar was master of Italy, Cato felt deep sorrow. He thought ruin was coming on the land, though he was mistaken. But still, he honestly thought Cæsar was doing no good to Rome and the Roman people; and, to prove his grief in the sight of all men, he would neither cut his hair nor shave his beard, nor wear a garland of flowers at a banquet or on a holiday. All his life long he had seldom laughed; now he was more gloomy than ever. Perhaps you think him foolish. But you must remember he was not gloomy on his own account. His heart was troubled for the sake of his country.

Pompey died on the shore of Africa, and his head was shown to Cæsar. Pompey's friend, Cato, also died in Africa. He had collected Roman soldiers and African allies about him, and he had made up his mind to fight Cæsar, and never to yield. His last stand was made at Utica (*U-tik-a*), a city near Carthage. He brought into this city large stores of corn; he mended its broken walls; he set up towers for watching and for defence; he had ditches dug round; he drilled the young men in the use of weapons, and in soldiers' exercises.

Meanwhile Cæsar came nearer the city. One midnight a horseman dashed into Utica, his horse all steaming, and brought the news that King Juba, the African, was beaten; that soon Cæsar would be at the gates.

Cato would not fly. He ordered that ships should be got ready in the harbor for such as chose to depart, and food was placed on board. From the shore he watched the rowers take the vessels out to sea, and the galleys retire into the faint distance, and he was left in Utica.

In the evening he read very deeply. The book he studied was written by the wise Greek, Plato. His sword used to hang over his couch where he lay. It had been removed by his son, who had a fear lest Cato should slay himself. On Cato discovering that the sword was gone, he asked one of his slaves the reason, and, not being satisfied with the answer, struck the slave such a blow on the mouth that he injured his own hand. I am sorry to have to tell you this incident, for it shows that Cato, with all his courage and faithfulness, was hard of heart toward his servants.

At length he regained the sword.

Through the night he sometimes read and sometimes slept a little; and as the birds began to sing at dawn he drew the sword from its sheath, stabbed himself in the breast, and soon afterward died.

I have already told you of another Cato. This one who died at Utica is called Cato the Younger.

TWO NOBLE BROTHERS

"HORROR! Two snakes on the bed!" shouted a Roman gentleman; and he was about to slay the reptiles.

"Stay, sir!" cried a slave. "Had you not better ask a soothsayer to tell the meaning of the strange sign?"

A soothsayer was fetched. He looked at the wriggling creatures, and, pointing to one and then the other, said:

"If you kill this one, you will soon die. If you kill that one, your wife will die."

The Roman reflected a moment. Then he killed the first one, and the second escaped. And soon afterward (so says the old legend) he died. He loved his wife Cordelia more than he loved his own life.

The good Roman's name was Gracchus (*Grakkus*), and his two sons were called the Gracchi. One was Tiberius (*Ty-beer-ius*), born in 168 or 163 B.C., killed 133 B.C., and the other Caius (*Ky-us*), born about 154 B.C., killed 121 B.C. They died some twenty or thirty years before Julius Cæsar was born. I will tell you a little about each.

TIBERIUS

He was elected tribune, or the people's man. Any one of the tribunes could stand up in the senate when a law was about to be passed, and cry "Veto!"— "I say no!"—and the law had to drop. Tiberius was a friend of the poorer Romans—the plebs, or commons. In early times, when land was taken from the foes of the republic, a good deal of it was divided among the people. And none might hold more than two hundred and sixty acres. On such an estate a Roman could live a healthy country life, and the yeomen, or small land-owners, who tilled these farms were stout and honest citizens, who loved the land which they made fruitful. But, little by little, the richer people (patricians) got the land into their own hands, and had it tilled by their slaves; and thus the hard-working freemen were becoming poor and unhappy.

In the forum, or meeting-place, at Rome there was a platform of stone raised eleven feet above the floor of the hall. Along the front of this platform (or rostra) were two rows of bronze beaks of ships captured from enemies in sea-fights. Tiberius would mount the rostra, and look down upon a crowd of the citizens, and say:

"The wild beasts of Italy have caves to crouch in, but the brave men who shed their blood for the fatherland have nothing left them but the air they breathe and the light of heaven. They have no houses, no settled homes; they wander to and fro with their wives and children. When a battle is about to begin, the generals bid their soldiers fight for the hearths which the household gods watch over; but, alas! these men have no hearths. The Romans make war to gain riches for the rich, and yet have no plots of land which they can call their own."

The people in the forum and in the poorer streets listened to such words with great joy.

The wealthy folk frowned, and murmured to one another that Tiberius must be hindered from stirring up the commons. They had secret talks with a tribune named Octavius. He promised to say "Veto" to any law that gave land to the plebs—the masses of the people. And so nothing could be done. Tiberius would step to the platform behind the ships' beaks, and speak of the happy days that would dawn when the plebs were land-owners. But Octavius was always there, ready to say "Veto."

The people were filled with wrath.

"No longer shall you be the people's man!" they shouted.

Octavius was thrust out of the office of tribune; the law for giving allotments of land to the commons was passed.

When Tiberius Gracchus had acted as tribune for one year he wished to be people's man again, though this was against the Roman rule. The rich patricians resolved that he should not again take office. His life was in danger. The night before the Election Day a crowd of his friends set up tents in front of his house to guard it against attack.

In the morning vast crowds of electors covered the slopes of the Capitol hill. They cheered wildly as Tiberius came in sight. But a band of his opponents forced their way toward him. Clubs and bludgeons were raised in deadly warfare. Men pushed hither and thither. Some hundreds of Romans were done to death. Tiberius was felled by a blow with a stool. A second blow crushed out his life. His body was flung into the river, and the people, cowed and beaten, mourned for their dead leader.

CAIUS

Now Caius, the younger brother of the brave Roman of whose death I have told you, was of a hotter blood than Tiberius. Indeed, he himself knew his temper was violent and his words oftentimes too strong. So he bade a slave carry a small ivory pipe, which, when blown, gave out a sweet and low note. Perhaps Caius was talking in a loud key.

"I tell you, gentlemen, that, as sure as I stand here—"

Then a gentle "Hoo-oo" would be heard from the ivory pipe, and Caius would drop into a lower tone!

Perhaps some of you girls and boys might talk more nicely if you heard the ivory pipe now and then!

After the death of his brother Caius lived for a while in a quiet manner, wishing to keep clear of brawls and tumults. But (so the old story goes) the ghost of Tiberius rose up before him in a dream, saying:

"Why do you loiter, Caius? There is but one way to take. Both you and I are fated to go that road. We must die the same death. Both of us have to suffer for the people's sake."

And so it came to pass that he took the side of the plebs, and they gave their votes that he should be a tribune, and for a time he had much power.

The plebs loved him. Once, when a show of gladiators was to be held in a public place in Rome, certain persons were allowed by the magistrates to put up stands round about, in order that seats might be let for hire. Thus the common people who could not afford to pay for admission would be shut out from the exciting scene of the gladiators in combat. Perhaps you will say that it was not right to set men fighting each other in that way. Yes, that is true; but the Romans had different ideas from ours. And if people were to see the show at all, it was not fair to permit only the folks with money to witness it.

Well, in the night the tribune, Caius Gracchus, led a band of workmen to the place, and bade them break down the stands. Next day the plebs found a clear space for them, and they enjoyed the spectacle of the gladiators, and praised the tribune.

You know that the Roman tribes were only part

of the people of Italy. The Romans were freemen and citizens. The rest of the Italians had no vote in the ruling of the republic. As we say to-day, they did not possess the franchise. Caius wished to give the franchise to the Italians. The patricians had no wish to give votes to so many more thousands of the common folk. They hated Caius.

A piece of land was chosen at Carthage, on the African coast, for a number of poor Romans to emigrate to; and Caius went to this spot to help arrange the new colony.

His enemies said he did his work badly, and he was summoned to a meeting on the Capitol hill to defend himself. Men's hearts foreboded an evil time. The night before the trial the friends of Caius guarded his door. In the morning his wife knelt, and held her son by one hand, her husband by the other, and begged Caius not to go to death. But he went forth like a brave man.

Angry tempers and angry words led to blows, and soon a dreadful massacre began. Caius was left with but three persons—one was his slave, the others were two faithful friends. The little party retreated to a narrow wooden bridge. The two friends defended the passage, and were cut down. Caius and his loyal slave died together in the Temple of the Furies, in the grove of trees just beyond the bridge.

The mother of the two noble brothers lived for some years afterward in peace in a country villa, much revered by all who knew her. A statue of her was set up, and on its base were carved the Latin words: *"Cor-*

nelia Mater Grac-chor-um"—that is, Cornelia, the Mother of the Gracchi.

TULLY

"YOU ought to change your name."

"My name is not a bad one!"

"No, but it is an odd one. Who would like to be called 'Vetch'? Vetch is food for cattle."

"Well," replied the man whose name was Vetch, "I will make my name glorious in the history of Rome, though it has a common sound."

In Latin the word for "vetch" is Cicero (*Sis-er-o*). It was the Roman Cicero, 106–43 B.C., who thus resolved to give glory to his strange name.

For a short time young Cicero had served in the army of Sulla, the Red General. He was not fitted for war. His form was slender, his stomach delicate. He attended the schools where grammar was taught, and also the art of speaking clearly so as to win the attention of listeners. This beautiful art is called elocution. It is the art of the actor and the orator.

Cicero's tongue charmed the Roman people. He was chosen first to one office, then another, and another, until he became consul. At that time a nobleman named Catiline, who had a fierce and reckless temper, collected twenty thousand men, and hoped to destroy the senate and set up a new government in Rome.

The Romans held a merry festival in the month of December, just as we keep Christmas. Some of Catiline's friends had formed a plot to set fire to Rome during the holiday-making. A hundred fellows had agreed each to take his station at a certain part of the city, and apply a torch to some wooden building, and so start a hundred blazes at once. And when the streets roared with red flame, and folk ran here and there in fear, the friends of Catiline would clash their arms, and cry aloud that a new power had risen in Rome, and there would be new governors over the vast empire from Spain to Asia.

But Cicero, the consul, was aware of the horrid plan. His spies brought word of all that went on in dark meeting-places. Five leaders were arrested, and a pile of javelins, swords, and daggers was found in a house, and seized in the name of the senate.

What should be done with the five conspirators? The senators met to consider. Nearly all judged that the plotters ought to die. Young Julius Cæsar rose and said:

"No; let us be merciful. Send these men out of Rome. Keep them prisoners, but spare their lives."

In his own heart he felt that Rome really did need new governors, though he did not think Catiline was the right man. The rich patrician families were no longer able to hold the mastery over the Roman world.

But Cicero was not of Cæsar's mind. He had the

five rebels brought out, and taken through crowds of people in the Holy Road (Via Sacra) and the forum, and so to the gloomy prison; and there all died at the hands of the executioner. It was now evening, and, as Cicero walked homeward with his lictors, the citizens ran at his side, shouting:

"Tully! Tully! The savior of Rome! The second founder of Rome!"

His full name, you must know, was Marcus Tullius Cicero, and he is often called Tully.

As the darkness deepened lamps and torches were fixed over doorways in all the streets. Many women went to the roofs of the houses and waved lights. Thus Rome was grandly illumined by the lamps of the people, instead of by the fires of Catiline.

The feelings of the citizens of Rome and the folk of Italy were like the ebb and flow of the sea, first rolling this way and then that—first for Cicero, then against him; then for Pompey, then for Cæsar. It was a time of change—a time of war and rumors of war. Cicero was banished from Rome for more than a year, and his houses were burned to the ground. He dwelt in Greece, but kept looking back to Italy with sadness and love. With much joy the people acclaimed him on his return; and, as a mark of honor, he was made governor of the mountainous land of Cilicia, in Asia Minor. And in that business he did right well. He made peace with the foes of Rome by wise dealings and without the spilling of blood. And he behaved justly toward the people of Cilicia. Unlike some other governors, he did not wish to tax the folk for his own gain.

The feasts which he gave were paid for out of his own purse. He kept up no vain show. No pompous footman stood at his gates to warn away the citizens who desired to see him; and he rose betimes in the morning, and was ready to speak with all who called at his house. Nor did he put any Cilicians to shame by causing them to be beaten with rods, or to have their clothes rent as a mark of his anger. Thus, when he left that province to go back to Italy, the people were sorry to say farewell.

You know there was a war between Cæsar and Pompey. It was a conflict of lions. But Cicero was no lion. He scarce knew which side to take.

"Shall I join Pompey?" he said to himself. "He is the better man. But Cæsar is a more clever statesman, and perhaps he will win."

So Tully chose the side of Pompey; and when Pompey was beaten, and soon afterward killed on the shore of Egypt, Cicero made his way back to Italy. Cæsar rode on horseback to meet him, and when he saw him, dismounted and ran to him, and embraced him, and talked to him as a friend.

But Cæsar was slain at the foot of Pompey's statue; and now what was to happen to Cicero?

Three men became three masters over Rome—Augustus, Antony, and Lepidus. Each had strong enemies, and they agreed to slay each other's enemies, and so rule in peace. Each wrote out a list of two hundred men whom he wished put to death. On one of their lists was the name of Tullius Cicero.

The dire news reached him that he was doomed, or "proscribed." At once he ordered his slaves to carry him in a travelling-chair, or litter, to the sea. He hastened on board. A fair wind blew. Soon he changed his mind, and ordered that the galley should make for the land. Then he walked with his little company of attendants some twelve or thirteen miles toward Rome, as if he hoped to see Augustus and touch his heart to pity. Again he changed his mind, and embarked on a ship, bidding the sailors voyage with all speed to a point of the coast where he had a beautiful villa. A flight of crows wheeled round the vessel, dismally croaking. When Tully was carried into the villa, and laid upon a couch, hoping to rest, the crows flew about the house, still cawing.

"This is a bad omen," whispered the slaves. "It bodes evil to our master."

They approached him as he lay on the couch.

"We fear this dreadful omen of the birds," they said. "We beg you to leave this ill-omened dwelling."

They placed him in the litter, and carried him toward the sea.

A band of soldiers had arrived, and were on the watch to take his life. They came to the house, and heard that he had escaped by the glade which ran through a thick wood. The soldiers ran round another way, and waited at the end of the woodland path.

After a time they saw the litter advancing through the shade of the tall trees. Cicero caught sight of the men in ambush. He knew his hour was come.

Silently he put his head out of the litter. The centurion, or captain of the band, beheaded him with a stroke of the sword.

Cicero wrote noble books.

One was on Friendship. A second was on Old Age. A third was on Duties.

He was a Roman, but his thoughts went over the world, and he said to himself that all the people in it were citizens of one earth. And so, in his writings, he speaks of men as "citizens of the world."

THE MAN WHO LOOKED LIKE HERCULES

A TALL, strong general, with large forehead, full beard, and a pleasant look in the eyes—such was Antony, who lived from about 83 B.C. to 30 B.C. When his soldiers stood eating at plain wooden tables in the camp, he would stand and take a share with them, and laugh and talk as if he were a common man of the ranks. And his men loved him for his free ways and cheerful temper. They admired his fine appearance, and said he was like the hero Hercules.

Antony was generous to his foes. Once, in a battle in Egypt, a person with whom he had been friendly was slain on the opposite side. No sooner did Antony hear of his old friend's death than he sent some Romans to search for the body. When it was found, Antony had it buried with a quite royal funeral.

To his friends he was even too generous, for he hated to be thought mean. Once he ordered his house-master (steward) to set apart a sum of money for a beloved companion. The steward placed the silver in a heap, and hoped Antony would change his mind, and give less. When Antony saw what was in the mind of the steward, he said, in a cool, stately manner:

"The amount is too small; double it, and take it to my friend."

In war he was ready to scale the walls of fortresses, to dash on horseback at the enemy, to endure hunger and thirst. When there was peace, he gave himself up to riotous living. The train of servants carrying his gold and silver vessels, etc., was a little army. They would set up his tent in a pleasant shady grove, beside a river, and lay a table as if in a palace-chamber. Tame lions would be harnessed to his chariot, so that crowds of folk would come and stare. He amused himself with actors and jesters. He would drink too much at a nightly feast, and sleep a drunken sleep the most part of the next day. Antony looked as strong as Hercules, and his body was indeed as manly, but not so his mind; he had not the strength to go without wasteful and selfish pleasures.

You have heard how Julius Cæsar died. After the death of Cæsar, his nephew Octavius (who was later the Emperor Augustus) fought for the mastery. Antony was beaten, and fled. His soldiers passed the Alps on their way to Gaul. So hungry were they that they were glad to chew the bark of trees. The general shared their coarse food, eating bark or roots or tough meat, and drinking unclean water, and making no complaint. Men flocked to him in Gaul. He now felt he was as powerful as Octavius and Lepidus. This Lepidus had been one of Cæsar's stoutest captains.

At last the three rivals met on an island in the beautiful Rhine river, and they talked and argued, and planned how they should divide the Roman Empire between them. The old Roman Republic was coming to an end. Emperors were now to hold the sway, instead of consuls, for some hundreds of years.

But Antony was not earnest enough to keep a grip on his share of the empire. He ran after pleasures as little boys run after butterflies. It fell to his lot to govern Asia Minor. He entered the city of Ephesus as if he came with a show for a circus. Women dressed as priestesses of the wine-god Bacchus (*Bak-kus*) and men attired like wild satyrs of the woods marched and danced in procession. And the streets of the city were crowded with noisy revelers who wore ivory crowns, and waved spears garlanded with ivy, and made merry music on harps and flutes and mouth-organs. Antony rode gayly amid the throng, and a roar of voices hailed him:

"Bacchus! Bacchus! ever kind and free! Yo! yo! Bacchus!"

Ah, but the hard-working people of Asia had to pay for all his follies, and many a poor cottager and artisan was forced to give heavy taxes to Antony's officers.

Making his way toward the East, he halted amid the mountains of Cilicia. There he expected to meet a lady of whom he had often heard, but whom he had never yet beheld. This was Cleopatra, the Queen of Egypt. She meant that he should see her in her glory, so she arranged to travel down a river to his camp. Her galley was a splendid boat: its stem was plated with gold, its sails were colored purple, and the oars were silver. Musicians played while the rowers rowed, and all kept time together. Under an awning of cloth of gold sat the lady of Egypt, fair as a Greek goddess, while maids who seemed to be lovely nymphs of the sea waited upon her, and pretty boys fanned her with long fans. The white smoke of incense curled over the galley, and smelled sweet. Multitudes of people ran along the banks of the river, gazing on the wondrous scene.

And when Antony saw her he loved her with a love that made him forget his own wife, and too often drew him away from his duty as a soldier and a Roman. When he stayed for a while in the city of Alexandria, at the mouth of the river Nile, wild and strange were his tricks and sports. At night he and Cleopatra would sometimes stroll through the streets, dressed as mere slaves, and act as if they were roysterers from a tavern.

One day Antony sat by a pool of water, fishing, and idle courtiers and ladies reclined in the shade of trees near by, and all the company were gay. Not many fish bit Antony's hook, and the queen smiled at his failure. So he bade a slave dive slyly into the water, and fasten a dead fish to the hook, so that Antony might appear to be catching something after all. This trick was repeated several times, amid the applause of the courtiers. But Cleopatra saw the deceit, and ordered one of her own servants to dive and fix a dried and salted fish to the lordly Roman's fishing-rod. Shouts of laughter pealed out when Antony drew up a fish that looked as foolish as it was salt. And Antony laughed at himself.

The next scene, however, was very different.

In this scene we find Antony once more a general, and leading his army of Romans into the far-off land of the Parthians. Often before had the Romans engaged in deadly struggle with these people of the East, and well did they know the terror of the Parthian darts. Antony was near to disaster more than once. His men were heroes. They marched a thousand miles into this savage district. They had to retreat through rocky passes, where no water was to be had. They beat off the enemy in eighteen fights. Antony lost twenty thousand infantry and four thousand horsemen. Thirst and sickness had killed many of these loyal soldiers. And when the army crossed a river which divided the Parthian region from Armenia, and they were free from the attacks of their fierce foes, they kissed the very ground for joy. But other troubles followed, for, in crossing the hills to the Mediterranean Sea, Antony lost some thousands of men in the deep snow-drifts, and through the bitter cold. In truth, he had not taken pains to carry on the war with care and prudence. He had hurried his men from place to place too swiftly, for he wished to get back to the Queen of Egypt. And thus he left his duty undone.

He had put away his wife as one whom he despised. The lady was sister to Octavius, and Octavius treated this act as a cause of war. In the port of Ephesus Antony placed his army in eight hundred and ninety ships, two hundred of these being sent by the queen. This huge fleet sailed to the island of Samos, and there waited for a while. All princes and governors in Antony's quarter of the empire were collecting heavy taxes, the money being dragged from the homes of the people in towns and villages. Many a heart was sore, because the war had taken the household savings. At Samos, however, enjoyment went on briskly. Stage-players and musicians amused the Court of Antony and Cleopatra, and roars of laughter were heard at the feasts.

Octavius brought his army across the sea to the coast of Epirus, opposite the western shore of Italy, and his navy prepared to meet the attack of Antony. The place of battle was called Actium. As Octavius went from his tent to the galley, he met a man driving an ass.

"What is your name?" he asked.

"Good Fortune."

"And the name of your ass?"

"Victory."

Glad was the heart of Octavius when he received this answer. It was a happy omen. He did indeed gain the victory, and a brass statue of the driver and the ass was afterward set up on that spot.

Antony's ships were large, and had on them big wooden towers, whence the men could shoot. About each large vessel of Antony's several of the ships of Octavius would gather close, and fighting went on furiously hand to hand.

In the midst of the tumult sixty ships suddenly left Antony's fleet. They were Cleopatra's. The queen was flying from the conflict. Antony again forgot his duty. He boarded a five-banked galley, and ordered the crew to sail in the track of the queen. He left his friends struggling, to live or die, as might happen. The queen raised a signal. Antony headed straight for her royal galley, and went on board; and the fleet sailed on to the south, and the noise of war was heard no more. Antony sat silent, his head between his hands. He felt ashamed and miserable. Neither he nor the queen spoke for a long time.

And so they came to Alexandria in Egypt. The stern victor followed. Soldiers and sailors alike deserted to Octavius. Antony saw that his cause was lost. He stabbed himself with a sword, and lay dying.

The queen had fled to a massive tower, where she had hidden her treasure of gold, silver, emeralds, pearls, ebony, ivory, and cinnamon. She and two women were alone. The dying Antony was borne to the gate of the fort. She would not open, but said that he should be hoisted on his couch by ropes to a window. The queen and her two companions strained hard at the ropes and drew him up.

> *Antony:* I am dying, Egypt, dying;
>   Give me some wine, and let me speak a little.

And as she bent over him he murmured that, if he must be vanquished, he was willing that a Roman should vanquish him.

> I lived, the greatest prince of the world,
> The noblest, and do now not basely die.
> Not cowardly put off my helmet to

My countryman; a Roman by a Roman
Valiantly vanquished. Now my spirit is going,
I can no more.
—SHAKESPEARE.

Thus he died. He had seemed so strong; and he was indeed strong in body. But he had not a strong will to go the way that was best for himself and Rome.

CAESAR'S FRIEND AND ENEMY

YOU remember how Brutus, Cassius, and other Romans of high position stabbed Julius Cæsar to death. Some people think that Brutus did well to help in the slaying of Cæsar. Others think he did evil.

He had been a friend of Pompey the Great. When Pompey had formed his camp, ready for the last struggle with Cæsar, Brutus entered as a friend. Pompey was much pleased. Instead of waiting for Brutus to bow low before him, he rose in the midst of his guards, and embraced the newcomer with much good-will. Brutus waited calmly for the trial of strength. The day before the battle of Pharsalia, while all the other men in the camp were talking of the fight that was coming, he sat quietly reading and writing.

Pompey lost the battle. Cæsar's Romans were clambering up the mounds that formed the walls of Pompey's camp. Brutus fled through one of the entrances on the opposite side to the storming party. A marsh was near. Amid the reeds he forced his way, his feet slipping in the pools of muddy water; and so he escaped. Not long afterward he wrote a letter to Cæsar, and became for a time his close friend.

160

But only for a time. Brutus hated the idea of one man, however wise, being lord of the Roman world, though I do not think he could have explained how so large an empire was to be ruled better. Many other Roman patricians had like thoughts. They urged him to resist Cæsar. He found papers laid on his chair in the senate-house, on which were written these words:

"Brutus, thou sleepest! Thou art not a true Brutus."

And, as you know, his was one of the daggers that killed the great general.

Nor did he care to submit to young Octavius, the nephew of Cæsar. He collected an army in the hill-country, north of Greece, and prepared for a trial of strength with Octavius. While marching to the attack on a certain town, he pressed forward a long way in front of the main body of troops, who were slowly trudging through the deep snow in the passes. The keen air of the mountains brought on a curious feeling known as the hunger-madness. No food was at hand; the baggage had been left far in the rear. His attendants then hurried on to the gate of the city, and begged for food of the very foes of Brutus. The citizens were men of a fine spirit, and handed out to the messengers some provisions for the use of Brutus. The city before long fell into his hands, but he remembered the kindness that had been done to him, and showed mercy to the inhabitants.

A different scene occurred at Xanthus, a city in Asia. Brutus had carried his troops oversea, and was seeking to band people together against Octavius. On his way he landed on the island of Rhodes. A crowd of the inhabitants cried out:

"Hail, king and master!"

"Nay," cried Brutus, "I am neither king nor master. I am the destroyer of Cæsar, who wished to be both!"

But then, as I said, he came to Xanthus, and there the folk had no mind to join him and help carry his eagles against Octavius. From village to village he had driven the peasants, and they had swarmed into Xanthus, and the Roman army had now begirt it with a terrible ring of power and death. Some of the Xanthians dived from the walls into the river that ran by. A multitude of them burst from the gates one night, and set fire to the machines (battering engines) which the Romans used to break the ramparts of the city. They were driven back. The flames spread from the engines to some wooden houses on the walls. A red light shot over the doomed town, and by its glare were seen men, women, and children hurrying from street to street, pursued by the stern Romans. But the people's soul fiercely fought against the idea of yielding to Brutus. They saw no hope in his rule and the rule of the haughty nobles who took his side, and who wished to make Rome everything, and leave the rest of the empire in slavery. They set fire to houses with their own hands, and then, with loud shouts of defiance, leaped into the dreadful flames and died for freedom! In one house Brutus saw the dead body of a woman, clasping her dead babe in one arm; she had set fire to her cottage, and then hanged herself sooner than fall into the power of the besiegers.

> . . . The foeman's chain
> Could not bring her proud soul under.

When Brutus and his comrade, Cassius, had subdued the lands of the East—in Asia Minor and Greece, and the islands round about—they prepared for the last tremendous clash of war. Octavius had come to Macedonia, and the two armies stood face to face at Philippi. The larger host was that of Octavius; but the legions of Brutus appeared more splendid, for their armor flashed with ornaments of gold and silver.

Two battles took place. In the first the horsemen of Brutus dashed with immense courage into the camp of Octavius, and plundered it. But the right wing of Octavius's army made a rush into the camp of Cassius, and bore all before them; and Cassius retired, and in his despair bade a servant strike off his head. The servant obeyed, and news was brought to Brutus that his comrade Cassius was dead.

The next day the conflict began afresh. The Romans who fought for Octavius were cold and hungry. Their tents had been sodden by heavy rains, and the camp, being on low ground, was damp enough at the best. A fleet from Italy, bearing provisions for their use, had been shattered in a fight with the galleys of Brutus.

Nevertheless, there was a stern valor on the side of Octavius which led to victory. His men had no trust that Brutus would govern the empire wisely for the good of all its people instead of for a few wealthy families. Some of Brutus's friends even went over to the enemy before his very eyes.

Soon the event was decided. A roar of voices, the thunder of cavalry, a hand-to-hand combat of footmen—and it was plain to see that the day was going against Brutus.

And now hear the brave tale of Lucilius. He was a sincere friend of Brutus, and when he saw that defeat was certain, and when he saw Brutus leaving the field, followed by a band of horsemen, he resolved to lay down his life for his friend. So he rode forward, and was at once seized. Being dressed in the style of an officer of rank, he was questioned.

"Who are you?"

"I am Brutus, the general."

"You must come with us to Octavius Cæsar."

"I pray you take me to Antony, for he will treat me more generously than Octavius."

They therefore led him to Antony. The deceit was soon discovered. They had brought the wrong man, and meanwhile Brutus had got safely away! However, no harm came to Lucilius. His life was spared, and he was treated with honor by the conqueror.

And what was Brutus doing?

With a small party of his officers he had ridden on till dusk fell, and the stars appeared. He halted in a glen where tall cliffs hung over a rippling stream. Here there was a cave in which he and his companions took shelter. They brooded sadly over the ruin of their cause, and wondered what would happen to Rome and to the patricians who had opposed Octavius Cæsar.

A helmet was dipped into the brook, and the water brought to Brutus, and he drank eagerly. Now and then noises were heard among the woods on the opposite bank of the stream. The enemy were searching for the defeated general.

Brutus felt that his hour was come. He spoke in a low tone to one of his friends. The man shook his head and burst into tears. A second did likewise, and others also refused to do what he asked.

He had begged them to slay him.

At length, one of them—a Greek—held a sword, and Brutus thrust himself upon it, and so died in the year 42 B.C.

Two great poets speak of Brutus in their verse; but while Shakespeare praises him, Dante (*Dantay*) condemns him.

Shakespeare, in his play of Julius Cæsar, shows the death of Brutus in the cave, and makes Octavius and Antony and their soldiers enter; and then Antony says:

> This was the noblest Roman of them all;
> All the conspirators save only he
> Did that they did in envy of great Cæsar;
> He only, in a general honest thought
> And common good to all, made one of them.

His life was gentle, and the elements
So mixed in him that Nature might stand up
And say to all the world, "This was a man."